BLACK GIRLS AND HOW WE FAIL THEM

BLACK GIRLS

AND HOW WE FAIL THEM

Aria S. Halliday

The University of North Carolina Press
CHAPEL HILL

© 2025 The University of North Carolina Press
All rights reserved

Designed by Patrick Holt
Set in Literata and Scala Sans
by Rebecca Evans
Manufactured in the United States of America

Cover art: Background © julijadmi / Adobe Stock; silhouette © Galina / Adobe Stock.

Library of Congress Cataloging-in-Publication Data
Names: Halliday, Aria S., 1990– author.
Title: Black girls and how we fail them / Aria S. Halliday.
Description: Chapel Hill : The University of North Carolina Press, 2025. | Includes bibliographical references and index.
Identifiers: LCCN 2024044996 | ISBN 9781469686103 (cloth ; alk. paper) | ISBN 9781469686110 (paper ; alk. paper) | ISBN 9781469683058 (epub) | ISBN 9781469687759 (pdf)
Subjects: LCSH: African American girls—Social conditions—21st century. | African American women in popular culture. | Girls, Black—Social conditions—21st century. | Misogynoir. | African American girls—Violence against. | Girls in popular culture. | BISAC: SOCIAL SCIENCE / Ethnic Studies / American / African American & Black Studies | SOCIAL SCIENCE / Women's Studies
Classification: LCC E185.86 .H253 2025 | DDC 305.48/8960730905—dc23/eng/20241029
LC record available at https://lccn.loc.gov/

To Alice's Sophia and all who have had to fight

SOMETIMES I GO MISSING

Sometimes I go missing, from myself.
I leave me behind in hopes of finding a piece, a peace of mind that I lost somewhere along the way.
I lost it after daddy chose violence rather than explanation or care.
I lost it after that boy forced me on my knees and my teacher asked what I was wearing when it happened.
I lost me when the boys, the teachers, the homegirls, the lovers, the family members, the people who said they loved me would rather I be silent than explain how they hurt me.
I lost me trying to please everyone because I was told that is what good girls do.
I lose me more when they reward me for taking care of others at my own expense.
So sometimes I go missing, from myself.
And I never know where she goes until I find her in a quiet place, hidden away from the world and from me.
I think she leaves when she knows I am not safe for her, when I choose to protect others instead of her.
Sometimes I go missing from myself and this time, I am not sure I will find her again.

—Aria Halliday

Contents

INTRODUCTION | 1
Failure Is Everywhere

CHAPTER 1 | 23
Hip-Hop's Daughters: Hip-Hop's Misogyny Problem Revisited

CHAPTER 2 | 43
Hypervisible Black Girlhood: Black Girls in the Obama Hopeland

CHAPTER 3 | 63
Loving Fast-Tailed Girls: *Queen Sugar*, Southern Black Girlhood, and Theological Abuse

CHAPTER 4 | 85
Black Girls Save the World

CHAPTER 5 | 107
Dispensable Black Girls: Throw Them All Away!

CHAPTER 6 | 129
Mean (Black) Girls

EPILOGUE | 145
Finding Healing in Failure

RESOURCES FOR FAILING LESS | 161
ACKNOWLEDGMENTS | 163
NOTES | 165
BIBLIOGRAPHY | 173
INDEX | 183

INTRODUCTION

Failure Is Everywhere

Jasmine Mans published a book of poetry in early 2021 called *Black Girl, Call Home*. Through a series of poems dedicated to exploring relationships with and between family members, siblings, ancestors, and communities in Newark and New Orleans, Mans explores life as a queer Black girl. Alongside poems such as "Witch" and "Fascinations," one of the most moving poems in the book is called "Missing Girls."[1] The poem is a word search puzzle, with the names of Black girls in the word list. The poem, although seemingly simple, bespeaks how Black girls are not found because they are not searched for. When we know their names, when we know that they are missing, Black girls can be found like a word in a word search. It profoundly indicts the lack of concern many have for finding Black girls and for the ways that the disappearance of Black girls is understood with apathy and seen as noncontroversial—as mundane as a word search. With Mans's book title, too, I consider the Black girls refusing to call home because home is not safe for them either. I also think about the ways I've been encouraged to make—and rewarded for making—my needs, desires, and complaints secondary to those of others. I have found this lesson of discontinuity within myself to be a disintegrating process, in which I become increasingly estranged from who I am. Whether missing or made missing, Black girls like me and those in Mans's poem cannot call home because of our collective refusal to see, know, or understand them as Black girls.

Black Girls and How We Fail Them is about Black girls and the discourses surrounding them that comprise the backdrop to Mans's "Missing Girls" poem and my own poem that opens this book. Inseparable from the Black girls who are missing in Atlanta or Nigeria, I explore how Black girls are seen and misrecognized across popular culture. Engaging cultural discourses on and social constructions of Black girls and girlhood through celebrity familial relationships and critically acclaimed films in popular culture, I theorize the ways that Black girls are treated culturally in the United States as a symptom of hatred that undergirds conversations about Black girls, cultural representations of Black girls, and Black girls' own lived experiences. Departing from scholarship about Black girls that has mainly focused on organizations and institutions that impact them, relationships that create difficulty for them, and Black girls' own theorizing of their experiences, this book focuses on the ideological work of cultural representation and how it is informed by Black girls' experience within organizations and relationships.

Black Girls and How We Fail Them is both a framework to understand how misogynoir—the specific hatred toward Black girls and women—metastasizes in our society through the images we consume in our leisure time and an indictment of the ways Black girls are treated by those who are supposed to love and protect them.[2] I frame these discussions through failure because of the ways that mass-produced, widely distributed popular culture promotes violence against Black girls. It is failure because we as individuals and as a society rarely choose to protect Black girls when we are given the choice. It is failure because we prioritize the feelings, egos, and futures of abusers, rather than the lives of those most vulnerable in our society. And understanding this failure allows us to see the mechanisms through which we can change.

I take seriously the premise that representation is not just about what we see but rather about the ways what we see communicates ideas about who we believe ourselves to be and how to interact with those who are not "us." As famed Black cultural theorist bell hooks theorizes, I, as a Black female spectator, read against and with the cultural norms that US society encourages audiences to use to understand representation.[3] I challenge myself and others who allow algorithms to "know" and suggest what we might like when we're scrolling on our phones or viewing devices, and I challenge how those choices curate misogynoir when we are simply seeking entertainment.[4] I locate complicity in misogynoir not just in the directors, casting professionals, actors, and producers but also in critics, award committees, viewers, educators, scholars, parents, and friends who are more readily equipped to notice the violence against girls and women when they are white. Whether written and directed by Black women or by someone else, the trope of Black girls as disposable is highly prevalent across genres and media types. This means, in turn, that the work we need to do to learn about and heal from misogynoir is for all of us. Yes, we are all failing. Therefore, I make explicit how we all fail Black girls, even as we attempt to create a less violent world for others.

The first step to laying bare our failure of Black girls is identifying how Black girls and girlhood are used in popular culture. In political, social, cultural, and entertainment spaces, Black girls and girlhood are used as discursive pillars. By this I mean that Black girls are positioned with or against others in discourses about problems and oppressions, but they're also used in deciphering best practices or crafting celebrations. Beyond the specific representations of Black girls that I examine throughout this text, it is important to describe the sociopolitical environment that surrounds Black girls and the choices that others make on their behalf. While I focus on twelve instances of failure, these only represent a small number of all possible cases and situations in which Black girls are mistreated in popular culture. Therefore, the discourses about Black girls alongside the films and narratives I feature in this book craft the cultural ideologies of misogynoir. They are a starting point and can be expanded to include new and old examples that I do not name. Across media types and different depictions of Black girls, I trace where our societal failure shows up through individual behaviors and collective beliefs.

In framing these cases, I considered how spaces of leisure and entertainment allow us to open ourselves up to and therefore become susceptible to hearing and therefore spewing misogynoir.

These discourses and representations are broadcast to us as entertainment, cementing the visual and spoken language of misogynoir, and we accept them as fun or unserious. The harm that they create is much more insidious because we assume it is only entertainment. Yet these very discussions construct the environment in which Black girls exist and ultimately serve as the background to when and why Black girls go unseen. Extending educator Tamara Butler's "Black Girl Cartography," which maps how and where Black girls exist in educational spaces, I mark some of the spaces within popular culture where Black girls exist.[5] My aim in Black Girls and How We Fail Them is to better situate Black girls' experiences within the popular culture representations and public discourses that further construct (and many times, narrate) their lives and provide some guidance toward creating a world that supports, affirms, and loves Black girls—all while equipping them to love themselves. Like Mans, I consider where Black girls are missing from our critical discussions of representation and how we have been complicit in depicting Black girls as unwanted and disposable, while letting Black girls fend for themselves.

Failing Black Girls: How Our Culture Cultivates Misogynoir

Politician Daniel Patrick Moynihan's 1965 report and Barack Obama's 2009–2017 presidency were decades apart in their agendas to shift US federal policy to support African Americans, but they agreed on one fundamental premise that has politically and socially narrated the experiences of Black girls and women. To address years of neglect and nihilism in Black communities, Moynihan and Obama argued for political focus on the social mobility of Black boys and men as the linchpin in elevating impoverished Black families to middle-class socioeconomic status. For Moynihan, the "virus" of racism could be staid by strong family structures, especially for poor Black people; his 1965 report hoped to propel federal obligations to Black people through building up Black men. Obama, similarly, constructed his 2014 My Brother's Keeper federal initiative with the ideological belief that Black boys and men, once bettered in community with other Black boys and men, could lift their families and communities out of poverty. Both argued that the lack of strong Black male role models contributed to violence, economic poverty, and family structures that relied on Black women and girls to take on a majority of household and community organizing labor. These ideas on their own provided ammunition for the many organizations and initiatives that support Black boys and men to flourish. Underlying these ideas, however, are narratives about fatherless Black girls and partnerless Black women who emasculate Black men by maintaining family structures while they are lost to juvenile and adult incarceration or murdered.

In both liberal and conservative ideologies of the family, children who lack fathers are subject to a life of terror. This is because those without fathers are not worthy of protection by anyone else; they are not appropriate liberal subjects—meaning they are beyond the patriarchal structure of family that dominates US discourse and are therefore perpetually uncivil. Cultural critic Imani Perry explains that our contemporary ideas about personhood (and protection) are based in philosopher John Locke's conceptions of sovereignty. She says,

> The family, heralded by a man whose wife, children, and chattel attended, was the basic social unit. The patriarch represented and led the family. He was the one possessed of full personhood. People to whom he was legally related as family (rather than as chattel) garnered ancillary benefits and partial benefits of personhood. The relationship between the patriarch and the members of his household was analogous to a king or parliament's reign over the nation, and later, post-monarchy, the patriarch was analogous to the nation itself, which possessed a form of legal personality, as well.[6]

Although Black people were not referenced in Locke's thinking (and perhaps are still not) on legalized descriptions of persons because they were considered chattel, both Moynihan and Obama structured their ideas about family and personhood through these definitions. To become a proper patriarch, they believe, Black boys must be prepared to take on their roles as patriarch through federally supported economic and social empowerment. Because the patriarch "represented and led the family" and "was the one possessed of full personhood," through his sovereignty as a person, he can provide "benefits of personhood" to all others in his family/kingdom. For our purposes, we should recognize that one of the benefits of personhood is protection; because others will recognize women, children, and chattel as belonging to a patriarch, they will be spared from the violence inflicted upon those who are not (or in the very least, there would be consequences for violence against them). Patriarchal protection is what keeps you safe, and when you are not recognized as a person (a.k.a. a patriarch) nor are you the property of a patriarch (wife, child, indentured servant, or enslaved attendant), you are not marked as valuable and therefore not worthy of protection. Therefore, Moynihan and Obama across two generations buoyed conservative and liberal political ideas about the so-called problems Black people face as intrinsically tied to the lack of patriarchal influence. It follows then that the people who need support to meet their full potential as patriarchs are Black boys and men, and the need for this support should come from all others in exchange for protection. This focus on Black boys and men has encouraged the belief that Black girls and women are not in need of assistance; this is a failure of priority. By suggesting that prioritizing Black boys and men alone will benefit all Black people, these agendas fail to see Black girls and women and fail to hold space for the specific gender and race (as well as class and sexuality) issues they face.

Beyond these two major political agendas that have encouraged economic and social attention to men and boys, the murders of Black men and boys have also pushed global support for policies and organizations that protect them. George Zimmerman's extrajudicial and highly prejudicial stalking and killing of seventeen-year-old Trayvon Martin in 2012 as well as the Ferguson, Missouri police murder of eighteen-year-old Michael Brown in 2014 propelled the United States in many ways, including the creation of the My Brother's Keeper program and the Black Lives Matter movement. The subsequent murders of Black boys and men in police custody or by general members of the population have also raised critical questions about the role of policing and the longstanding contentious relationship between communities of color and those who police them.

Activists as well as legal scholars like Kimberlé Crenshaw and organizations such as the African American Policy Forum and the Georgetown Law Center collectively noted the erasure of Black girls and women who have also been murdered in policing discourse. Through campaigns based on the social media rallying cry #SayHerName, Black girls and women encouraged the acknowledgment of those who had been murdered, like Renisha McBride in 2013, Sandra Bland in 2015, and Atatiana Jefferson in 2019. Because of its social media virality, however, this rhetorical move to prioritize Black girls and women became a portable marker for all people murdered by the police or extrajudicially—recognized with new slogans like #SayHisName and #SayTheirName. While I do not fault those who saw #SayHerName and its viral popularity as an opportunity to also propel the names of others slain into popular parlance, the new markers indicated the continued erasure of Black girls and women from political discussions and national organizing, bespeaking the lack of care that US society has for those who are Black and femme.

I have argued elsewhere that the lack of attention to Black girls' specific experiences have led to them being subsumed into the theorizing and political organizing of Black women.[7] Likewise, literary scholar Habiba Ibrahim helpfully argues that in Black feminist scholarship of the 1970s and 1980s, "black girlhood marked a site from which one might transition into an alternatively human subject, having rejected the properly humanist conditions attributed to white male adulthood. As such, black girlhood was imagined as the site of a socially capacious political project."[8] This means that even in

Black feminist scholarship, some of which is still considered timely despite our temporal distance from when they were writing, Black girls and Black girlhood are utilized to make sense of others' aging, attitudes, life expectancy, and familial commitments. In how Black girls are both socialized and theorized, we have relied on their latent reproductive possibilities, making them unformed Black women. Black girls are known, especially in historical narratives, as those approximate to Black womanhood because of the ways enslavement both ungendered and de-aged them. However, our commitment to Black girls in the contemporary period has continued to advance sluggishly. This is a failure of commitment.

In many cases, we see Black girls as always violable, yet always at fault for the outcomes of those who really deserve support.[9] Despite alarming statistics that recognize both the intimate and the social experiences of Black girls, the framework for understanding Black girls' experiences still heavily relies on seeing and reading them as not-yet Black women, potential mothers, premarried partners—always almost something rather than who they are. By maintaining Black girls' political and social proximity to Black womanhood, we render them invisible and perpetually unknown as Black girls. Beyond the ways that Black womanhood is seen and theorized, rendering Black girls unknowable unless in proximity to womanhood is itself also misogynoir. Our inability to see, understand, or theorize Black girls as girls makes us just as culpable in their continued dehumanization in schools, in political spaces, and in our homes. This is a failure of recognition that the media makes more concrete.

Talk to/for Me: Black Talk Radio and Black Girl Misogynoir

A major factor that has contributed to contemporary misrenderings of Black girls are celebrity-run and hip-hop-based talk shows. With the rise of hip-hop culture on the national and global stage since the 1980s, Black discursive space has found its home on large radio-based platforms. Thanks to the widening of media opportunities due to the advent of the internet, Black discursive spaces have also popped up on every social media platform, especially YouTube, Facebook, and Instagram. Since the murder of George Floyd and Breonna Taylor in 2020, these opportunities have expanded even more and allowed more people to host platforms such as podcasts to discuss Black popular culture and political issues. Two of the most popular shows are the hip-hop radio show *The Breakfast Club* and the celebrity- and self-help-focused Facebook podcast *Red Table Talk*. Both shows have reached a fever pitch in terms of popularity on social media and in discussions at barbershops, beauty salons, and Black community events, yet they use misogynoir to maintain the millions of listeners they garner each episode.

Created in 2010 and nationally syndicated since 2013, *The Breakfast Club* radio show—indeed the "world's most dangerous morning show"—is a New York–based show dedicated to hip-hop culture, Black political issues, and cultural commentary on dating and relationships presented by the hosts DJ Envy, Angela Yee, Charlamagne tha God, and daily special guests. Inducted into the Radio Hall of Fame in 2020 with reportedly 8 million listeners, *The Breakfast Club* provides a platform for Black artists, political figures, and popular discussions to thrive. Beloved by some, the show takes seriously the messiness and spectacle of celebrity and encourages special guests to reframe gossip or "set the record straight" in their interviews. Since 2014, the radio show has also been recorded on camera and has subsequently become viral on social media for its celebrity gossip-related interviews. Most of these interviews, however, revolve around the disrespect of Black women celebrities. From Nicki Minaj and Remy Ma to Nia Long and Monique, Black women who are interviewed on *The Breakfast Club* are regularly asked about their sexual experiences, their relationships, and their political affiliations rather than whatever consumer products they planned to discuss.

The questions regularly position social media gossip as factual or craft false dichotomies to purposely force confrontation. Particularly around issues relating to sexuality, dating, and relationships, *The Breakfast Club* hosts provide new opportunities to shift cultural discourses, but they rely on misogynist, homophobic, transphobic, and ableist "gossip" to cultivate listeners. This forces guests into hostile discussions, positioning themselves against unnamed adversaries, unconfirmed rumors, and antagonistic social media posts. For Black women, Black femmes, and Black queer men, the hostility directed at them not only voices the animosity they experience every day, but it also uses the masculine bravado and overrepresentation on the show (via Charlamagne and DJ Envy) as a vehicle for misogynoir. Even when guests of more masculine gender expression challenge the hostile environment created by gossip-laden questions and disrespect-imbued commentary, the hosts and the subsequent social media commentary about the interviews depict the artists as being childish or silly.

Because of its cultivated and dedicated audience, The Breakfast Club continues to create hostile interview environments in the name of hip-hop journalism. In hopes of prompting social media virality, they disrespect the very culture they say they wish to promote. And yet, as one of the only publicly accessible outlets for Black and Latinx hip-hop listeners to learn about cultural discussions and new ways to engage with their beloved artists, the show continues. Even as Angela Yee, the only female host on the show, exited in 2022 and celebrated getting her own morning show, she also reflected on facing misogynoir from guests, fans, and others in the industry. The Breakfast Club's success has led to various other shows hosted by celebrities, such as Red Table Talk, that chronicle discourses that parallel and intersect hip-hop culture.

The advent of Red Table Talk, the Daytime Emmy–awarded Facebook Live series, extends Black talk radio conversations for those who use social media as their main news outlet. Modeled on kitchen table conversations held by women across generations, actress-producer Jada Pinkett-Smith; her mother, Adrienne Banfield-Norris; and her daughter, artist Willow Smith, together record and produce conversations that they have had about mental health, beauty and hair, love and relationships, and pain and trauma. When Red Table Talk first aired in 2018, it was built around inviting guests to their table to "be real" about issues they are facing, though the hosts have delved into their own issues as a celebrity family several times, too. The show has garnered over 20 million views because of the authenticity that audiences perceive from conversations that include insights into the hosts' lives and struggles as well as controversial social media topics, providing opportunities for other celebrities to address rumors surrounding their lives. However, the proximity of the Smith family to many of the celebrities they invite on the show, as well as to their own family gossip, further maintains allegiances to misogynoir. Guests and the hosts (especially with the inclusion of Will, Jaden, and Trey Smith on various occasions) present a so-called authenticity that is as curated and circumscribed as any other reality television or talk show.

While *The Breakfast Club* uses social media gossip to press guests into confrontational topics, *Red Table Talk* presents their discussions as equally real yet highly curated because guests respond to social media posts and questions that have been cleared before any discussions begin. *Red Table Talk*'s "realism" is built on the hosts' and guests' ability to curate their antagonism, even at a table that is presented as a feminine and therefore supposedly safer space, yet the show still relies on objectionable and stereotypical ideas about race, gender, sexuality, religion, and family. Beyond their experiences and background information provided surrounding the show, the journalism supposedly occurring is built on turning social media discussions into newsworthy information.

These curated discussions built on the US cultural obsession with celebrity and the belief that social media presents authenticity fuel the popularity of both shows. Despite their popularity for different reasons and with different audiences (although there is overlap in justification and audience), both *Red Table Talk* and *The Breakfast Club* further ingrain problematic assumptions about Black women, Black femmes, and Black queer people that ultimately mystify the systems and discourses that leave Black girls unprotected, but for the sake of social media likes.

Although not explicitly interviewing Black girls, both *The Breakfast Club* and *Red Table Talk* represent environments where our beliefs about Black girls are created, cultivated, and shared because of how Black girls are discussed on the shows. In discussing violence, mental health, family dynamics, new popular media, and other topics, these talk radio shows allow narratives about Black girls (especially their sexuality and value) to construct critical discourse within Black communities about who is important, worthy of protection and love, and why. Alongside these discourses, and those cultivated by Moynihan, Obama, and other political spokespersons, Black girls' worthiness and cultural importance is intrinsic to the rise of slogans and organizations that highlight so-called Black girl magic.

Black Women's Labor: The Intellectual Work of Black Girls Code and Black Girls Rock

In the past twenty years of public discourse, there has been an uptick in the prevalence of Black women working to rehabilitate their image through mental health podcasts, real estate workshops, "boss bitch" business seminars, and the revitalization of community organizations dedicated to bettering their lives and communities; these developments extend the work of Black women's social and political organizing dating back to the early twentieth century. Through educational, political, social, and pop cultural means, Black women's commitment to shifting public discourse about them, their bodies, their desires, and their love interests have propelled a cultural reckoning. This shift recasts previous generations' knowledge and idioms as Black cultural wealth, laying the groundwork for Black women to navigate the world through their own Black political consciousness. The national push for Black hair to be included under nondiscrimination legislation, the rise of products in big-box departments stores by and formulated for Black women, and the popularity of Black women-focused festivals like EssenceFest illustrate decades of work by Black women in multiple spheres to make inclusion a reality rather than just an ideal. Revealed as the most educated population by a National Center for Education Statistics study in 2020, contemporary Black women much like generations past have found ways to shift their own ideas about themselves but also US societal beliefs about them.[10] These shifts in public discourse about Black women attempt to supplant centuries of narratives that present Black women as inferior, ugly, asexual, angry, and reckless. Through these avenues, Black women have been invested specifically in developing counternarratives about who they are and of what they are capable when supported, acknowledged, and celebrated.[11]

Newer initiatives such as Black Girls Code (BGC) and Black Girls Rock! further the work of Black women's clubs, sororal organizations, and political activism not only to highlight the ingenuity of Black women but also to create pipelines through which Black girls can access better-protected spaces. Because of the prevalence of misogynoir in all areas, Black women have always cultivated opportunities to celebrate and uplift each other in Black woman- and girl-centric spaces. Although different in scope, Black Girls Code and Black Girls Rock! both aim to provide visible recognition of Black women's and girls' cultural importance, alongside other initiatives in politics, education, and public health to encourage Black girls and women as well as raise awareness.

Emerging alongside US societal conversations about diversity, inclusion, and change in major industries, Black Girls Code formed in April 2011 as "the girl scouts of tech."[12] Founder Kimberly Bryant cites her daughter's misogynist experience at an engineering summer camp as the catalyst for BGC and Bryant's mission to create learning environments that center Black girls and other girls of color in technology. Bryant argues that by teaching girls of color to code through a chapter-based web and app development program, BGC can shift the discourse about Black girls' abilities and provide the opportunity for Black girls and their communities to see themselves as creators. Because Black girls are "natural change agents," Bryant contends, "we teach one girl to code, they will teach ten more."[13] Despite recent turmoil within the organization's leadership, Black Girls Code is the foremost site of Black girls' technological skill. Bryant considers the group revolutionary, much like the protests and radical rhetoric of her childhood in 1960s Memphis, Tennessee, and she therefore believes providing technological advancement for Black girls will not only increase their awareness of tech jobs and skills but also present new economic opportunities.

The discursive environment of Black Girls Code forces the tech landscape to acknowledge the lack of representation of Black women in tech positions by providing a pipeline and early access engagement with Black girls who code for companies like Google and Meta (formerly Facebook). However, this access does not address the misogynoir that many within tech companies believe and develop their company cultures around. Much like academia, medicine, law, politics, and other industries, Black women are not underrepresented due to their lack of knowledge about these fields or their lack of motivation or skills. The belief that Black women are unassimilable to white corporate cultures and that companies need not address the racist and sexist behaviors of managers and employees push out Black women. While I applaud Bryant's attempt to address the lack of technological skill that Black girls may have due to lack of opportunity even in tech hubs like San Francisco, I contend that we must still address the discursive environment in which they attend college and/or begin working. Those environments rely on the interplay of racist and sexist (as well as other oppressive) principles seen and experienced by Black girls and women in representational entertainment industries.

DJ and model Beverly Bond's organization Black Girls Rock! attempts to award and acknowledge Black women within sport, music, and other entertainment industries. Before Cashawn Thompson coined the phrase "Black girls are magic" or #Blackgirlmagic in 2013, Beverly Bond considered the necessity of acknowledging Black women's success in an awards program that heralded "owning our magic, rocking our truth."[14] Originally conceptualized as a t-shirt that Bond could use to celebrate Black women who were underrecognized in US society, given her own experience with being maligned, the idea broadened into a DJ academy for Black girls that would not only teach them the skills needed to embrace hip-hop music and culture but also celebrate the Black women who were regularly shifting US culture through political activism, music, sport, and other industries. Awards like "Star Power," "Young, Gifted, and Black," "Living Legend," and "Trailblazer" solidify the night of glamour and Black women's empowerment that has been airing on BET (Black Entertainment Television) since 2010. Since its first ceremony in 2006, Black Girls Rock! has expanded to a Black girls' enrichment and mentorship program, a book club, a festival, and a TV channel, unveiling a program called "Black Men Rock!" in 2022 during its festival in Washington, DC.

Taken together, Kimberly Bryant and Black Girls Code alongside Beverly Bond and Black Girls Rock! transform the negative experiences of Black women and girls into opportunities for them. The rise of both programs not only bespeaks the sociopolitical shift in the possibilities for Black women to communicate about their experiences in the public sphere, but it also funds opportunities to change those physical spaces for Black women and girls not yet in those spaces. Their existence also co-constructs narratives about Black girls since their aim is "Black girls" rather than just Black women. In their names, they rhetorically state what Black girls do as both a celebration and world-building assertion; by this I mean that Black girls are perhaps celebrating on their own, but more accurately, their doing ("code" and "rock") is what makes them worthy of celebration. Developed by Black women for Black girls, the organizations Black Girls Code and Black Girls Rock! and the discursive environment they create around Black girls require that there is a doing that allows celebration—that Black girls by way of Black women either learn to code(switch) to engage in a career in technology or find an industry that is visible enough that makes them celebratory. The representational politics of who gets celebrated or even the cities where Black Girls Code is available maps where Black girls can be seen, heard, and celebrated. Outside of those spaces, where do Black girls exist? And what kinds of Black girls are worthy of being noticed?

Together, the political agendas, the Black cultural discussions, and the Black girl-focused organizations and discourses that have arisen since Barack Obama took office in 2008 construct the cartography of Black girls' contemporary representation. Betwixt these cultural touchpoints and beyond the ways that Black women construct Black girls' discursive and physical worlds, Black girls are subject to people who hold these ideas of their subjectivity and personhood. They are supposed to be useful, hypervisible yet invisible, and subject to others' concerns and thoughts always. They are supposed to learn and do in service of celebratory praise, if only from Black women. While others are identified as people who are deserving of love, support, affection, encouragement, and protection, Black girls are told directly and indirectly that they are not safe, not valuable except for someone else's evolution or power, and should not be seen until they are acknowledged. Therefore, *Black Girls and How We Fail Them* attempts to make this representational map visible, demarcating where and how Black girls are exhibited by others as well as where they challenge how they are told to exist.

Mapping Our Failure of Black Girls

Black Girls and How We Fail Them is structured through the practice of finding Black girls. Each chapter examines aspects of Black girls' experiences through cultural discourses and across types of popular culture, petitioning us to move away from a focus on those who talk about and harm Black girls to the Black girls themselves. These spaces initially present Black girls as only seen through their association with parents and abusers, then eventually as sexually advanced. These presentations of Black girls from daughters of important and powerful people to hypervisible political pawns and fast-tailed girls structure how Black girls are seen in film, the focus of later chapters, and act as the sites that I believe could be most impactful for Black girls' healing. In presenting where Black girls are seen across various popular culture examples, I follow the failures Black girls experience to illustrate the interconnected relationship of anti-Black girl discourse, abusive and manipulative behaviors, and outright failures to protect Black girls of any age.

In chapter 1, "Hip-Hop's Daughters," I theorize the ways that hip-hop's culture of performed misogynoir translates to the ways that Black men artists publicly treat and discuss their daughters. The failure to hold men accountable for their mistreatment of the girls and women in their lives has created a culture of mistrust and abuse. I explore three global hip-hop artists-turned-moguls—Shawn Carter, a.k.a. Jay Z, Sean Combs, a.k.a. Diddy, and Clifford Harris, a.k.a. T.I.—whose relationships with their daughters have been the focus of both controversy and praise. Lauded by some as the "ultimate rap dads," these men represent the best of hip-hop's authenticity, sexual prowess, and economic acumen, while also the ways that misogynoir is part and parcel of the quintessential (and considered the most authentic) hip-hop aesthetic. Despite their popularity, these men equally represent the biggest controversies in the past five years regarding their treatment of Black girls and women in their lives as well as the figures through which Black men coming of age in the 2000s and 2010s made sense of their new status as fathers. I illustrate how hip-hop's problem is not just one of misogynoir through music videos and lyrics, but rather a cultural disgust of Black femaleness that their so-called authenticity carries over into their relationships with their daughters. Hip-hop's daughters, then, represent how the push for legibility for Black men and masculinity within hip-hop has required misogynoir that goes beyond the stage.

Building on the use of misogynoir within parent-child relationships, chapter 2 focuses on Sasha and Malia Obama after their parents' exit from the White House. "Hypervisible Black Girlhood" explores how Black girls exist in a constant state of surveillance and control. Black girls are subject to public concerns about their sexuality, their bodies (especially if they are pretty or not), and their futures, which turns their friends into reporters and their choices into indictments of their parents' (especially their mother's) ability to rear them. While articulated alongside invisibility for Black women, hypervisibility for Black girls is tied to age-old concerns about representations of blackness that rely on ideas about Black girls as future "race women."[15] By studying the Obama girls as the future of our collective investment in inclusion, equality, and prosperity that surrounded their father, I frame the fascination and subsequent horror with their private lives as a culture of surveillance. Expanded beyond family and friends through contemporary social media platforms, this culture of surveillance is honed on Black girls to control rather than protect them. Defying cultural norms of misogynoir, however, Black girls refract this surveillance with their own control of the public eye and self-possession.

"Loving Fast-Tailed Girls," chapter 3, theorizes the cultural landscape that constructs and defines a self-possessed Black girl as a "fast-tailed girl" and the ramifications of this concept. I bring together Black feminist ideas about the "fast" girl to clarify the structure of how everyday and fictional Black girls—especially dark-skinned, southern, and Christian—are mistreated, abused, and ignored through compounding surveillance and violence. The concept of the "fast-tailed girl" is based in theological, white supremacist, and misogynist ideas of Black female sexuality that is appropriated by Black people—men and women, parents, and strangers alike—to control Black girls. Framed through social media discourses and the high-profile case of singer Robert Kelly, I illustrate how Black girls are treated in the same spaces where they should be safe. This chapter lays the foundation for how the beliefs we have about Black girls and how we talk about them across public media translates to how we fail Black girls within popular films.

By locating the girls who have been harmed in the discussions, abuse, and surveillance of our culture, *Black Girls and How We Fail Them* unfolds a web of misogynoir at work in entertainment as well. Available on streaming services like Netflix, Amazon Prime, and Disney+, and highly regarded for their cinematic depictions of Black girls, the six Hollywood films from 2012 to 2020 I feature in chapters 4, 5, and 6 illustrate three popular presentations of Black girlhood: salvific Black girls, dispensable Black girls, and mean Black girls. Whether in futuristic, dystopian, or everyday cultural landscapes—all of which I consider fantastical realism—Black girls are represented in ways that continue to circulate misogynoir.

Discounting Black girls' feelings, self-esteem, and needs, these films illustrate alarming ways that the mistreatment of Black girls in fictional and real-life situations are normal and therefore justified. I engage this conundrum represented in all six films: the factors that encourage others to choose Black girls as saviors are the same factors that present Black girls as mean and dispensable. Whether by parents or guardians, friends, or potential romantic suitors, Black girls are taught to be useful or be left behind.

In chapter 4, "Black Girls Save the World," I explore the representations of Black girls in dystopian environments in *The Girl with All the Gifts* (2016) and *Beasts of the Southern Wild* (2012). Marked by the failures of the adults around them, the Black girls in these films illuminate how Black girls are assumed to be saviors. Asked to sacrifice themselves and ignore their needs or desires for others, the Black girl characters—Melanie and Hushpuppy—in this chapter show the enormous burden that Black girls carry in societies that are dying, damaged, and left them to die due to the poor choices of adults. Black girls are supposed to fix economic, environmental, and social disasters, especially at their expense.

The following chapter, "Dispensable Black Girls," focuses on the Black girls who lead *Project Power* (2020) and *A Wrinkle in Time* (2018). Both dealing with chaos, loss, and fear, the Black girls in these films are faced with Black men who are readily willing to dispose of them because they are not acting in ways that they want. Extending larger constructions of Black masculinity that are built on the demonization of Black girls and their needs, these films illustrate how Black girls' safety measures are regarded as disrespectful and reasons for their mistreatment. Robin and Meg, girls struggling to create a sense of normalcy despite losing parents, friends, and safety, show us the difficulty Black girls face to protect themselves from the very people who are supposed to protect them. They are dispensable when they go against ideologies of Black masculinity that encourage selfishness and self-centered decision-making.

In chapter 6, I focus on the advent of what I call the "mean Black girl" and how fear and insecurity are characterized as mean and headstrong for Black girl characters in *Selah and the Spades* (2019) and *Cuties* (2020). Feared by others and represented as going against cultural norms and their friends, Selah and Amy encourage us to consider the ways Black girls are not allowed to speak about or show their insecurities except through meanness in popular culture. While both characters are redeemed through self-acceptance, the portrayal of insecurity and fear as meanness for Black girls reinforces cultural attitudes that adultify and dehumanize them, challenging the ways they express themselves and the cultures that encourage them to take charge of themselves and others.

Concluding with an epilogue, *Black Girls and How We Fail Them* turns to a discussion of healing for Black girls through community accountability. I center Black feminist theories to map what healing looks like for Black girls amidst cultural constructions that position them as fast, mean, and dispensable. I consider what Black feminists tell us about healing and how centering our strategies on Black girls will reverberate across space and time. I close this book with the call for a collective commitment to healing through failure and share what that has meant for me. I believe that change occurs when we realize both the problematic ways we operate with ourselves and each other (failure) and also the promise that self-care (healing)—literally caring for self by setting boundaries, naming the people who harm us, and being accountable when we are the ones named—can create a more just future for us all, but especially for Black girls. How we get free starts with claiming our failures and being accountable to the way we harm others and ourselves. Contemporary popular culture via streaming platforms and quick-moving social media like TikTok allow us the opportunity to mass-produce and globally distribute a different commitment than that of violence, hatred, and abuse. By identifying the cultural discourses, the cinematic representations, and the failures that we have committed against ourselves and the Black girls in our community—all things that contribute to the violent experiences of Black girls that pervade popular media representations—I believe we can find those that are missing, including ourselves, and start anew.

Our political landscape, our entertainment, and our communities have cultivated abusive, highly surveilled, and anti-Black girl environments. We have embraced failure through misplaced priorities, loose commitments, and misrecognition. We have taught Black girls that safety is only for those that they should protect. We have made our interpersonal spaces as well as public conversations and entertainment hostile to Black girls' feelings, desires, and bodies. By mapping how we have failed through our use of misogynoir in the conversations we have about Black girls and the images we circulate about them, *Black Girls and How We Fail Them* attempts to locate Black girls, uncover why they have been missing, and show how we can bring them home. Given the global popularity of the genre and the great potential available since its fiftieth anniversary in 2023, let's start with the culture that I love and that has failed Black girls arguably the most—hip-hop.

CHAPTER 1

Hip-Hop's Daughters

Hip-Hop's Misogyny Problem Revisited

> For too many black men there is no trust, no community, no family. Just self.
>
> —Joan Morgan, *When Chickenheads Come Home to Roost*

For some, Jay Z's *4:44* album was a watershed moment in hip-hop and in Black men's public relationships with Black women. He raises concerns about not only the ways that he interacted with and hurt his wife, Beyoncé Knowles-Carter, but also the ways that he disrespected women in the past. In the title track of the album, Jay Z apologizes repeatedly to his wife and the women in his life. He explains his behavior as result of his lack of emotions and refusal to love them as they tried to love him. He refutes years of bravado in his music in the song "Family Feud," when he directly challenges the notion that wealth comes from money. He says, "A man that don't take care of his family can't be rich," not only following the logic that family is the most important thing, but noting that without one a man could never be rich. This type of commentary in *4:44*, in many ways, brought up discussions for Black men and women about the (mis)trust and hurt that shapes their relationships and daily interactions. As he states on the album, Jay Z became willing to make these public pronouncements of his failures based on his inability to love or be there for his wife when his daughter, Blue Ivy, was born.

Calling up lines from his song "Beach Chair" from the album *Kingdom Come* a decade prior, Jay Z realizes how important his daughter is in his development—"I got demons in my past, so I got daughters on the way." This line in the song not only cites the problems he had in the past but also posits that "daughters," whether figurative or actual, would be the consequence. Culturally, daughters generally hold this interpretive resolution for promiscuous men, as if some biological causality for their countless infidelities means they will have daughters so that they will have to come to terms with the harm they've caused to women through their relationships with their daughters and desire to protect them from men like themselves. Beyonce's song "Daddy Lessons" on the *Lemonade* album follows a similar corollary; as fathers, Black men can teach their daughters to be weary of men like them—men who refuse relationship, commitment, accountability, or remorse. Whether these songs are fictional or not, the maturation of men is built on the pain of women and their maturation occurs because of the birth of their daughters. However, the maturation of men does not eliminate harm.

By focusing on dynamics among hip-hop, misogyny, and father-daughter relationships, I am interested in how Black girls learn who they are and who will love them based on Black men's performances of masculinity in hip-hop. Hip-hop masculinity's focus on sexual prowess means that everyone should disregard the girls and women that are used to undergird it—a failure of both care and accountability. In *When Chickenheads Come Home to Roost* (1999), hip-hop journalist Joan Morgan explicates the pain Black girls experience when their fathers disappear. Morgan argues that she (and girls like her) learned to passionately love their fathers based on the fear of him leaving, inadvertently teaching her later that violent behavior, sexist language, and being emotionally or physically unavailable was just "the way men are."[1] I find her argument about the love patterns Black girls learn from their fathers particularly pertinent, especially in the realm of hip-hop culture and what she has called the hip-hop generation. I consider what lessons Black girls learn from their fathers about the men they will encounter in (heterosexual) romantic couplings.

Recognizing, as music scholar Mark Anthony Neal explains in *Looking for Leroy* (2013), "that the most 'legible' black male body is often thought to be a criminal body and/or a body in need of policing and containment—incarceration . . . thus 'legible' black male bodies, ironically, brings welcome relief, a comforting knowingness casually reflected in notions like 'niggers will be niggers' (a distinctly gendered term)," I center the ways that the legibility of Black masculinity in US popular culture hinges on the preoccupation with authenticity, women, and material objects as if intrinsic to masculinity.[2] In particular, the obsession with realness in hip-hop among the Black men rappers that dominate its creation processes is crucially linked to the ways they perform fatherhood, particularly as fathers to Black girls. Despite their increasingly global cosmopolitanism, rappers-turned-moguls like Diddy, Jay Z, and T.I. continue to shape their public personas in the digital age through their relationship with their children. What does it mean when "real" men in hip-hop transition from being philanderers and emotionally unavailable partners to fathers of Black girls, younger versions of the women they claim to love but use, victimize, and abuse? I am thinking here about how Shawn Carter (Jay Z), Sean Combs (Diddy), and Clifford Harris (T.I.) have had public conversations regarding their daughters and the women in their lives that illuminate the ways that Black girls exist in hip-hop cultural spaces.

While artists, critics, and fans position the birth of a daughter as "a powder keg moment" for their transformation into manhood, Black men like Carter, Combs, and Harris illustrate the cultural misogynoir that is spearheaded by Black men in their interactions with Black women and with their Black daughters.[3] I focus on the interviews, music, and digital presences of these global icons over the past five years and the ways that they continue their sexist and problematic relationships with Black women in their relationships with their daughters. Black girlhood, as experienced by their daughters, is majorly shaped by these men and their refusal to see Black girls beyond the ways they have seen their Black women sexual partners or the so-called fast Black girls they once knew.

Structures of Patriarchy: What Is a Fuckboy?

In *When Chickenheads Come Home to Roost*, Joan Morgan argues that hip-hop/rap provides a necessary vantage point for understanding the gender dynamics in the Black community. Morgan contends that while "sistas are hurt when we hear brothers calling us bitches and hos," "the real crime isn't the name-calling, it's their failure to love us—to be our brothers in the way that we commit ourselves to being their sistas."[4] Morgan's argument pushes past the more basic consideration of misogyny in hip-hop being the use of "bitches" and "hoes," and instead cites concern at the lack of relationship, of trust, of love that Black women feel from Black men. She cautions Black women to not give up on their relationship with Black men because ultimately a man cannot give what he does not feel for himself, especially when "there is no trust, no community, no family. Just self."[5] The real issue of misogyny in hip-hop is the selfishness that is promoted and cultivated within and beyond the music and culture. Morgan's understanding of hurt and lack of trust is built fundamentally on the kin-like connection and sibling relationship that Black men are taught to spurn and which they therefore fail to cultivate in relationships with Black girls and women.

Contemporarily, this refusal to build relationships with women has been characterized with the term "fuckboy" (or in Black spaces, "fucknigga"). While the word in its original usage is based in African American/Black vernacular to describe a "bitchass nigga" or a man who does fake or strange (or, even effeminate) things, it has evolved to mean a man who refuses to acknowledge his or his partner's emotions; he playfully dismisses any discussions or declarations of commitment although he strings women along with platitudes about their connection; he seeks out women he can use for sex, emotional support, or economic favors; and when confronted about his habitual lack of commitment and false promises, he gaslights her or victimizes himself, dismissing accountability for any wrongdoing.[6] While this kind of man (or woman) is not new, the concept of the fuckboy has gained traction within the last decade to specifically address men that perform these behaviors and/or that used to act in these ways but through a maturation process no longer do. The real problem of the fuckboy is self-centeredness based in a refusal of intimacy and lack of accountability—byproducts considered privileges of patriarchy in wider US culture. In this way, Black men's selfishness, cultivated within hip-hop spaces, is emblematic of a global phenomenon of patriarchy. Culture critic Imani Perry explains the creation of the Western world and the legal construction of a person as the building blocks to modern patriarchy; Perry argues, "The patriarch was created through three juridical forms: sovereignty, property and personhood" and was enacted through "theaters of patriarchal domination" in the public domain.[7] Patriarchal domination, generally, is enacted against those who are considered nonpersons and therefore have no rights, like those rights patriarchs have or which patriarchs should respect. Outside legalized contracts, which can only be entered into by patriarchs, patriarchs are not required to respect the sovereignty or rights of nonpersons—what Perry calls "performances of nonrecognition."[8]

Although Black men were not originally included in the sphere of patriarchs, they now regularly perform patriarchal domination over "nonpersons" like women, children, effeminate or gay men, and men without other types of property (chains, cars, etc.) within the public domain of hip-hop as well as other spaces. Whether used as props to illustrate Black men rappers' prowess, legacy, and adherence to capitalist exploitation, women and children within the empire of hip-hop are considered accessories despite their consistent contributions to the music and culture. Symptomatic of many cultures, hip-hop's patriarchs are claimed as the true progenitors, the so-called real creators, and the ones to whom hip-hop culture is passed (from man to man, as when Snoop Dogg and Dr. Dre crowned Kendrick Lamar the king of West Coast rap, or even father to son, as in the case of producer DJ Khaled, who gave his son producer credits at the tender age of four months), despite how many women are involved or how many women labored on, suffered for, or assisted with the art that these patriarchs create.

These men provide the commentary on the skills and prowess of new men and the lack of skills or so-called substance of women who enter the space; they also teach their peers and younger men how to create estates that mature with them as they age. Some women rappers (especially of the late 1990s and 2000s) have performed "a sort of patriarchy by proxy" that further promotes Black men's patriarchal status, further contributing to Black men rappers' stature.[9] Regardless of fictional or real claims as "the best in the rap game," Black men rappers craft the narratives and lifestyles within which women, other men, and children are reduced to strings that they can pull at will. Chastising relationship intimacy, responsible fatherhood, sexual monogamy, and life purpose beyond "money, cash, hoes" (as Jay Z says ad nauseam in his 1998 song), Black men rappers craft a system of patriarchal domination that replicates the performances of nonrecognition and intimacy aversion typical in the global white-supremacist capitalist patriarchy we all live in. This microcosm of larger society maintains highly gendered discourse perpetuating ideas about the "subjugation of females and the feminine, whether such language emanates from the mouths of men or women."[10]

As men loosed from accountability and intimacy, fuckboys wreak havoc. Whether or not all men participate in activities that disregard emotions, dehumanize women and children, or promote hypermasculinity through ideologies of conquest and empire, the logic of the fuckboy permeates the culture of hip-hop and other cultures that overlap it. Even while some Black women rappers (extending the work of Black women in blues, jazz, and other genres) speak plainly about the sexism within hip-hop spaces, I have found that the fuckboy culture of hip-hop extends beyond the music into the hearts, minds, and relationships of Black men through the way that Black women's music is purported to be lesser than (labeled in contemporary descriptions as "pussy rap"), the way that Black men rappers construct them as video vixens rather than authentic emcees, and the way their relationships with men (and women) are portrayed.[11] These men focus on themselves, shirking the responsibilities of community and causing harm to the other men, women, and children with whom they are supposed to be in community. Even when they transition to fatherhood, many of these men cling to patriarchal dominance that they learned within hip-hop spaces. They are guided, in their transitions from fuckboys to fathers as well as in their continued misogynist relationships toward women, by some of the most famous Black men rapper-producers: Jay Z, Diddy, and T.I.

"Big Pimpin" to 4:44: Jay Z and Black Men's Misogynoir Maturation

Heralded as one of the best rappers alive and the "ultimate rap dad," Jay Z/Shawn Carter represents the quintessentially stereotypical Black male experience.[12] As a New Yorker who grew up selling drugs in a housing project with an absent father, Jay Z's career has chronicled his desire for wealth, sexual prowess, poverty, issues with his parents and family, love, and recently fatherhood. Jay Z's shift from Big Pimpin' Jigga Man to 4:44 maturity has been particularly important in his cultural shift within hip-hop spaces. While "'03 Bonnie and Clyde"—his first song with Beyoncé—positioned his monogamous relationship with Black pop princess Beyoncé Knowles as the ultimate power couple, the fifteen years of public performances and interviews of their relationship has codified for many Black women the idea that even the most beautiful and most talented of us (as represented by Beyoncé) will be heartbroken and cheated on. Jay Z's infidelities (and Beyoncé's miscarriages, pregnancies, and performances about those topics) with "Becky"— a pseudonym for other women both he and Beyoncé use—triggered twin public discourses about Black men's ability to be faithful in a monogamous relationship and Black women's seemingly required ability to forgive and forget experiences that leave them emotionally tattered. Beyond the controversies of their relationship that became centerstage in 2016 with the release of Beyoncé's *Lemonade*, fostered in 2017 with Jay Z's 4:44 (considered a response to topics and ideas in *Lemonade*), and supposedly settled with their joint reconciliation album *Everything Is Love* in 2018 under the stage name The Carters, I am more interested in the ways that Jay Z's narrative in *4:44* provided the evidence required to become the posterchild for Black fatherhood, particularly to Black girl children. With the birth of daughter Blue Ivy in January of 2012 and twins Rumi and Sir in 2017, Jay Z has subsequently interviewed on various occasions about how he had to mature and be the kind of father he never had.

Whereas his men interviewers pointed to the ways that his infidelities and Beyoncé's heartbreak alongside Blue Ivy's birth provided the necessary ingredients to mature him and make him the rap dad (and billionaire) he is celebrated as today, theologian Candice Marie Benbow's "4:43" notes the wear and tear on Black women that emotionally unavailable and harmful Black men cause when she says, "I wonder if you realize the cost we pay for loving men like you. My anxiety. Bey's miscarriages. My cousin's hair loss. Your homegirl's weight gain. Depression. Suicidal ideation. Substance abuse. Retail therapy and maxed credit cards. Entertaining niggas we don't even like just to feel wanted. So many forms of self-harm. We pay with our bodies. Sometimes our lives."[13] Benbow lays out the multiplicative ways that Black women and their bodies suffer, while men like Jay Z mature and grow. Black women in this way are the fertilizer to Black men's emotional and psychological maturity, even when they are just girls as Beyoncé was when she first met Jay Z.

Jay Z admits this growth potential at the birth of Black daughters and Black mothers' emotional casualties, and he subsequently receives validation for it from other men and some women. Like narratives of Black girls described as fast or whorish in service of Black men's unchecked libidos, ideologies like these position Black girls' fracturing and emotional distress as the necessary ingredients for Black men's maturity and adult well-being.[14] As daughters, Black girls feel the brunt of households emotionally torn by Black men's immaturity and infidelities through their own feelings of abandonment and lack of self-esteem, while Black men and boys get to celebrate their newly erected maturity at Black girls' and women's expense.

Beyond individual households, the misogynoir that undergirds Black men's emotional growth is bridged in their relationships with other men. Benbow's article further establishes the idea that men like Jay Z are in community with other men, who all benefit from Black girls' and women's self-harm. She argues, "You are part of a nation of brothers whose selfishness-turned-growth always leaves someone wounded ... I long for the day when a woman's strength isn't measured by how much shit she takes from a man as deeply as I yearn for a time when the growth of men doesn't require broken hearts, shattered dreams and pounds of flesh."[15] Even in his interview with David Letterman—in which Letterman recounts all the likenesses between his life and Jay Z, calling them "twins" and noting his own issues with infidelity as a nightmare that he had "almost blown up [his] family"—Jay Z notes that for a lot of men, there is a low "emotional IQ" and that the tools that are available for boys and men stop at "stand up, be a man, man up, don't cry."[16] Letterman (who admittedly avoided marriage as long as possible) and Jay Z bond over their infidelities and the ways that their wives stood by them, and therefore, they learned to develop emotional tools that made them better husbands, fathers, and men.

In his lyrical study of Black men rappers and parenthood, Matthew Oware argues that alongside the predominance of sexist and misogynist lyrics, a small percentage of lyrics from popular rap artists from 2004 to 2009 presented them as "decent" but "imperfect daddies."[17] Juxtaposed with Black women artists who "questioned the fidelity and responsibility of Black males," these artists held "positive views of the idea of family and their family role," while also characterizing Black women as "untrustworthy and materialistic."[18] While lyrics are not solidly indicative of Black men rappers' feelings (especially as Jay Z notes that rap pretends to be biographical and rappers are just storytellers), pop culture scholar Richard Iton is able to locate the "blueprint for the remasculinization of the texts of black politics and the community's public spaces" as far back as Public Enemy's 1987 and 1988 albums, which claimed the "banishment of women (and some men) from black deliberative arenas" and bound hip-hop generally "with the preservation of masculine privilege, youth, heterosexuality, lower-income status, and to some extent Islam."[19] Said differently, the narrative Jay Z describes in 4:44, which articulates a shift to understanding his role as a husband and father and developing emotional acumen while his wife grieved multiple miscarriages and then finally birthed their daughter, is built on a sonic history of Black men rappers who use Black women as props for their masculinist identities (while calling them untrustworthy gold diggers) and their children as the conduits to understand themselves as "decent" men. This sonic history, or nation of brothers as Benbow calls them, manifests a legacy in which Black men rappers who eschew accountability and responsibility through countless infidelities and emotionless relationships cite Black women as untrustworthy then use the harm they have caused as the infrastructure for their maturity and decency.

Collectively, Black girls' and women's own mental, emotional, and physical well-being are the host for Black men's parasitic growth. Black men can hold each other accountable or speak about growth and apologize, as Jay Z does in 4:44, because of the "stillborns" and lost "innocence" that Black women suffered. The myriad interviews Jay Z has done as a result of 4:44 and his performance as a now mature and emotionally available man, husband, and father are direct conduits through which the propaganda of "boys will be boys" progresses into manhood; men are allowed to use Black women's "broken hearts, shattered dreams and pounds of flesh" and their daughters' issues with abandonment and people-pleasing habits as the birth of their mature selves and do interviews on the late-night talk circuit and in magazines to cement their popular reputation as decent yet imperfect men. Jay Z, as a rap-artist-turned-billionaire mogul, has relationships with other Black men, like Diddy and T.I., who are fathers and have actively benefitted from their relationships with their wives and significant others, as well as their relationships with their daughters. Bedfellows based on the women they use, the secrets of how to use them, and the business models they have used to shape their capitalist endeavors, men like Jay Z, Diddy, and T.I.

produce a "bro code" of mechanisms to harm Black girls and women to in turn bolster Black boys' and men's individual and collective maturation.

Mogul Daddy Diddy: Fuckboy Antics

A fixture in the hip-hop and global music community for the past thirty years and considered a mogul for his multiple musical groups, production titles, restaurants, and other ventures, Diddy (also Love, P Diddy, Puffy, Puff Daddy, Sean Combs) represents a ghetto-fabulous musical tradition that highlights Black men's ambition and capitalist success. Like Jay Z, Diddy's economic growth over the past three decades has facilitated his contemporary positioning as a family man alongside high-profile relationships. Although his relationships with singers Jennifer "JLo" Lopez and Cassie were highly public, his relationships with model Kim Porter and designer Misa Hylton Brim resulted in his initiation into fatherhood. He is presently father to seven children; he has four children with model Kim Porter—Quincy (whom Diddy legally adopted), Christian, and twins D'Lila and Jessie—as well as Justin (from his relationship with Misa Hylton Brim), Chance (from his relationship with Sarah Chapman), and Ava (a white formerly homeless girl, whom he announced that he adopted on Instagram in spring 2020). Particularly after the sudden death of Kim Porter, popular news quickly captured Diddy as a grieving soulmate. Although Porter had been separated from him for over a decade and led a career of modeling and acting, her association with Diddy overshadowed all other aspects of her life and death (for example, her only Wikipedia entry in 2023 is as a note within Diddy's personal life). Her untimely death also precipitated his public positioning as a full-time doting father and provider for his large family, for which he was featured on the May/Mother's Day 2019 cover of *Essence* magazine. Despite this posturing and public celebration of Diddy's hip-hop fatherhood, Sean "Diddy" Combs is a fuckboy-turned-father.

In an interview with *Essence* in 2006, Porter and Combs discussed their "unordinary" love as well as his infidelities. Described as hip-hop's Jay Z and Beyoncé before they were coupled, Porter and Combs were together from 1994 to 2007 (with a break from 1999 to 2003). They noted their deep connection despite the lavish, self-centered bravado and lifestyle that Combs rapped about or promoted in his music videos. In 1999, while Porter and Combs lived together, and shortly after Porter gave birth to their son Christian, news broke that Diddy and Jennifer Lopez were in a relationship. Porter recounts that Diddy's relationship was "so public, so humiliating, so disrespectful" and hurt her immensely.[20] But she says, somewhat glibly, that her phone never stopped ringing: "He was calling fifty, sixty times a day" and ignored her wishes to be left alone. Porter says, "He was very, very intrusive."

According to Combs, his relationship with JLo was supposed to galvanize Porter to be more lavish in her affections; Combs argues that the thing that drew him to Porter made him feel less secure in her attraction since she was reserved—"I'm used to walking in to applause."[21] While Combs seems to have matured after the threat of being jailed on weapons charges in 2001, Porter was still wary of his advances because of publicity surrounding his relationship with JLo. The interviewer recounts that Porter's "biggest fear is that if it happens again the relationship will be over," citing the possibility not only that it could happen again but also that Porter would not be as forgiving a second time.[22] Combs playfully encourages the reporter to end the piece discussing the possibility of marriage for Combs and Porter; he says, "You should end the piece like that . . . with me talking about getting married. It'll give hope to all the girls who fell in love with a player . . . make that ex-player." Six months later, Porter officially called it quits with Combs; as Porter awaited the birth of their twin girls, stylist Sarah Chapman gave birth to Combs's daughter, Chance. Porter's biggest fear became a reality.

While Combs and the women in his life have portrayed unity about the children he has fathered concurrently, the overlap of his relationships with Lopez, Porter, Chapman, Cassie, and others signals less than harmonious couplings. Porter, often cited as his "soul mate," tells Essence in July 2007 that her relationship with Combs faltered due to lack of trust in his fidelity. She says, "I left because at this point in my life I want something different for myself. I invested ten years, I have children, and I've always stood by him. But now it's time for me and what I want to do for Kim. . . . We're committed to our children even if we couldn't commit to each other."[23] Porter's comments highlight not only why she decided to end the relationship but also that issues with commitment despite time and children precipitated the breaking down of their connection. Porter's language denotes investment, reproductive labor, and loyalty—all behaviors that Black women especially are supposed to uphold in characterizations of love in hip-hop music and culture despite any issues with fidelity or return on investment from the men to whom they are attached. The narrative of the "ride or die" lover is specifically gendered for women in heterosexual relationships—regardless of what occurs after they fall in love with a "player . . . ex-player" like Combs, they must always be loyal to their men.

Despite how many children he may have, Diddy's inability to commit to a woman whom he calls his best friend, even as he says trust bonded their relationship, is quintessential fuckboy behavior.[24] In her exclusive with the Combs family after Porter's passing, producer dream hampton foments his use of Porter's body, emotions, and time when she says, "Privately, Kim helped Puff grow into a better man and father."[25] Porter actively created the chrysalis, even in death, that Diddy has used time and again to reproduce himself over the years (potentially corresponding with his many name changes). Calling his shift to full-time father as "mommy mode," Diddy says, "Before this, I was a part-time father, you know? My family was always first, but there are countless times when I chose work over everything else."[26] While he acknowledges how Porter's death now requires that he become more involved in his children's lives, the gendered use of "mommy mode" relays how the daily physical, emotional, and educational well-being of children is decidedly a woman's domain. Still somehow, Diddy's admission of choosing music over his family as well as putting fatherhood on the backburner, for years, is recounted as a love-centered fathering project both by hampton (a Black woman) and in *Essence* (a magazine dedicated to Black women). Diddy then goes on to cite how Porter dealt with the death of her own mother as the blueprint for how his daughters have taught him how to grieve; strangely, her grief after losing her mother somehow taught him how to grieve his so-called soulmate and former lover—framing Porter as a mother-like figure to Diddy. From his relationship with Porter and learning how to deal with grief from his daughters, the Black women and girls in Diddy's life created the safety net and the proverbial village that have allowed this "bad boy" to grow into a man, making countless mistakes, maturing, to emerge a celebrated father on the cover of a women's magazine dedicated to the lives of Black women, for Mother's Day.

While Diddy's business acumen is celebrated for the high fashion brand recognition, his work within communities across the United States, and his status on who's who lists, the foundation for his work and his continued success is the bodies and tears of Black women and girls. Whereas 4:44 represents Jay Z's acknowledgment of and apologies for the hurt he's caused the Black girls and women in his life in the process of his maturation, Diddy's *Press Play* relays his desire for mature love. The album was released in 2006, the same year as the birth of his daughter with Chapman and the end of his relationship with Porter. Despite his five-year hiatus from music-making, Diddy's lyrics on the album are irritatingly self-focused, with every song highlighting his financial status, his prowess, and the types of women he likes. He continually calls himself "a king," "the [American] dream," and "a boss" throughout the album, likening himself to Donald Trump and Michael Bloomberg. Like Trump and Bloomberg, and his friend Jay Z, Diddy's public ethos is that of his moniker "bad boy."

Started in 1993 by Diddy, Bad Boy Records has become not only synonymous with him (due to his regular use of the phrase in songs) but also a mimesis of societal ideas about who bad boys are and what they do. It is not a coincidence, then, that Diddy and Porter were likened to Bobby Brown and Whitney Houston, nor that Diddy's last comments about his relationship with Porter in 2006 mentioned how their relationship served as a model for women who had fallen in love with a (ex-)player. Despite the rosy remaking of Diddy in *Essence* and elsewhere, there has been no public reckoning with his fuckboy behavior or its casualties. Diddy refuted multiple lawsuits alleging sexual assault, rape, sex trafficking, as well as physical and verbal abuse by Cassie and two other unnamed women in a December 6, 2023 Instagram post, "Let me be absolutely clear: I did not do any of the awful things being alleged. I will fight for my name, my family and for the truth." He later was accused of similar activity by producer Rodney "Lil Rod" Jones in February 2024.[27] His statements come on the heels of multiple companies severing ties with him and streaming platform Hulu cancelling plans for a reality television show about him and his children, called *Diddy+7*.

No matter the amount of musical and fashion projects with his sons or magazine editorials with his daughters heralding his fatherly ways, Diddy is even less evolved than his fuckboy-turned-father hip-hop counterpart, Jay Z. As Black men from similar familial and geographical backgrounds, sharing visions of capitalist empires that benefit Black men and socialize in similar circles, Jay Z and Diddy also share connections to one of the most popular fuckboy-turned-father rappers, Clifford "T.I." Harris.

Hymen Hysteria: Black Men's Fake Fatherly Concerns

Like Diddy, T.I.'s fatherhood became part of his public persona within the past decade with the 2011 start of his reality show, *The Family Hustle*, which features his longtime partner, Tameka "Tiny" Harris, and their children—Major, King, Heiress—as well as his children Deyjah, Domani, and Messiah (and Tiny's daughter, Zonnique, from a previous relationship). T.I. and Tiny Harris were married after almost a decade together, and a year before the show launched. Along with their blended family of seven children (to match Diddy's seven), the Harris family also experienced a stillborn pregnancy after complications. Their reality show provides a public platform for the multitude of ways that misogynoir plays out in their family dynamic, yet T.I.'s profound fuckboy behavior was illustrated with his oldest daughter, Deyjah Harris. T.I. is emblematic of southern Black fathers and their relationships with their daughters, an embodied and personable misogynoir, an extension and interpersonal representation of how the world treats Black girls.

When T.I. joked about protecting his daughter by having an obstetrician check that her hymen was intact every year before she turned eighteen, the overwhelming response was negative. However, he decided to do an interview with *Red Table Talk*, a Jada Pinkett-Smith talk series exclusively posted on Facebook, to discuss his position. T.I., with Tiny's verbal support, made it clear that his previous comments were a joke and that Deyjah's mom accompanied him as part of a regular doctor's visit when Deyjah was fifteen or sixteen years old. He pivoted to discussing control and how as a father his job is to guide and advise, which can only occur with some amount of control. Pointedly he says, he desires to protect his daughter from "all of the slimy, grimy, chubby fingered, little boys who want to just come and defile and destroy the sanctity that I have [protected thus far]."[28] Whereas his tone was again playful when he said, "defile and destroy" (hence the laughter that he received from Jada and her mother Adrienne Banfield-Norris), he doubled down on the need to protect his daughter from boys who have "animalistic urges" to make sure she will "keep her expectations low" so she doesn't "get her feelings hurt." He goes on to say that virginity, particularly for girls, is indicative of childhood and once "you lose your virginity . . . you must heighten the level of responsibility." He argues that sex is an adult decision and if a child makes that decision, they should be held to a higher level of responsibility and figure out what they plan to do in other aspects of their life. As he talks, Tiny is visibly uncomfortable and her facial expressions communicate discontent with his comments; however, she does not speak. Tiny's refusal to speak may indicate that she feels less inclined to speak about T.I.'s relationship with his daughter since she isn't her mother, but her facial expressions hint at discontent with the ways her husband treats and talks about Black girls.

Like Diddy and Porter, T.I. and Tiny also discuss how many of their issues stem from infidelities and lack of trust.[29] While T.I.'s tone and words continue to communicate joviality during the interview, the more he jokes, the more Tiny is visibly emotional about the public "fun" he has had and its subsequent harm to her. She works to stay composed and communicate the hurt she felt as he sought solace in other women's arms after returning from prison; Tiny even admits that she "never ever ever had sex with anyone" during their marriage, and T.I.'s response, said in an incredulous and joking manner—"I never ever ever lied"—communicates not only the differing approaches to their relationship and serious discussions of harm but also the publicly acceptable responses that men and women should have to infidelity.[30] Tiny's statement and further explanation of how things changed with her developing her own voice and "standing on [her] own two feet" after he went to prison indicated that T.I. was both domineering in his control of his longtime partner and that she—as Jada Pinkett-Smith explains—agreed to relinquish part of herself to please her partner and be taken care of. Despite women like Tiny "being a good woman" and "holding it down" while T.I. was incarcerated, she was rewarded with more infidelities. Similar to how Beyoncé correlates her miscarriages to Jay Z's infidelities, Tiny seems to attribute her stillborn daughter to stress and havoc wreaked by her beloved. And yet, as they say in the interview, only after the loss of their daughter was marriage possible.

For most people, T.I.'s public remarks and behavior regarding his relationship with his daughter Deyjah and his wife Tiny indicate a lack of maturity and understanding of Black girls' and women's experiences. However, T.I.'s continued public guffaws are propelled by misogynoir—especially in southern Black Christian contexts— that refutes Black men's responsibility for chaos, while blaming Black women for the so-called failures between Black men and women as well as the Black family. While celebrated for his business acumen—like his mogul counterparts—his life philosophies regarding control, fatherhood, and intimate relationships attenuate Black girls' and women's autonomy, self-confidence, and expression. Said differently, his and other Black men's approaches to life and their own emotional maturation are predicated on the need to vilify then discard Black girls and women, which in turn creates the "most unprotected women" that he claims to protect (harkening to a 1962 Malcolm X quote about Black women being the most disrespected and unprotected women in US society). Men like T.I. disguise their fuckboy behavior as self-protection or nonchalance, falsify the harm they've caused as necessary ingredients to their own maturation, and then publicly downplay it, while gaslighting the girls and women about whom they say they care.

Fuckboy Fatherhood: A Regime That Must End

T.I.'s loss of a child, multiple infidelities and experiences within the prison system, and public discourses he has output as a lay philosopher—particularly around issues that Black men face (at the expense of discussing the harm they cause the Black girls and women in their lives)—braid his experiences and presentation with those of Jay Z and Diddy. Together, these hip-hop moguls propel Black cultural discourses that impact the quotidian experiences of Black women and girls. Though they represent different aspects of hip-hop culture—whereas Jay Z and Diddy are New Yorkers, T.I. is distinctly southern and Atlanta rap—they signify a generation of Black men who came of age in the 1990s and 2000s and shaped much of the cultural discourses and attitudes about Black girls and women that permeate society today through their music and public behaviors. Their behavior, now as mentors in the ways of longevity in hip-hop, encourages men like rapper Kiari "Offset" Cephus (who has consistently disrespected his union with fellow rapper, Cardi B, then apologized through lavish gifts and stalking) and rapper/producer Daystar "Tory Lanez" Peterson (who shot fellow rapper Megan Thee Stallion in 2020 then continually gaslit her on social media and encouraged a questioning of her sexual preferences as an indictment of her character), while the listening public disregards their behavior in the name of good music. Their previous behavior and present metamorphoses as fuckboys-turned-fathers emboldens other Black men to use the Black girls and women in their lives as the fodder for their evolution toward maturity.

While hip-hop is not the only space in which misogynoir is encouraged, hip-hop and its moguls like Jay Z, Diddy, and T.I. can majorly change how Black girls and women are treated. They could shift the ways that Black girls are seen and heard as self-determined, and rightfully in need of support and protection by Black men, by first accepting responsibility for the harm they've caused to all hip-hop's daughters. Beyond new music and lyrics that revisit their "bad boy" behaviors, these men could illustrate what maturation can look like for Black men—especially those who have needed therapy in order to make sense of their past. Jay Z, Diddy, and T.I. can model behaviors that protect Black girls and women, that manifest self-awareness and understanding for Black boys and men, and that mend intimate partner violence through social discourses about Black men's responsibility to themselves and to the women they love.

While hip-hop daughters are obscured, other Black girls become visible, born of the strife and success of their fathers, when the patriarch needs them to shore up his fatherly evolution and honor within cultural discourses. Extending my discussion to include surveillance via the media, I explore the frenzy surrounding former president Barack Obama's daughters, Sasha and Malia, in the next chapter. Because Black girls are always already perceived as fast and are protected only by the honorable declarations of their fathers, Sasha and Malia represent how hypervisibility of Black girls is used to surveil them but also to justify patriarchal dominance. Their public correction through misogynoir justifies the need for (Black men's) patriarchal violence toward Black girls, using their behaviors to illustrate the failures and successes of patriarchal dominance.

CHAPTER 2

Hypervisible Black Girlhood

Black Girls in the Obama Hopeland

> These narratives about Black women and Black girls being sexual objects—those are old. Those are hundreds of years old stereotypes that are actually used in purpose of keeping Black women and Black communities in a particular space.... We have more technology now than ever and we have more inequality and injustice to go with it.
>
> —Safiya Noble

> From the moment we begin to navigate the intricacies of adolescence, we feel the weight of this threat [violence against women], and the weight of contradictory expectations and misguided preconceptions. Many of us begin to put too much value to how we are seen by others. That's if we are seen at all. The issue is even more intense for Black women, who struggle against stereotypes and are seen as angry or threatening when we try to stand up for ourselves and our sisters. There's not much room for passionate advocacy if you are a Black woman.
>
> —Megan Thee Stallion

During Barack Obama's presidency, some people were cautious about embracing his version of blackness and the ways that he upheld Black masculinity as a presidential nominee. At the same time, many were taken with the Obama family—specifically Michelle Obama and the Obama girls—because of their perceived unapologetic blackness born of the South Side of Chicago and working-class origins. Michelle, Malia, and Sasha represented the advancement of Black women and girls in ways that had yet to be seen contemporarily. Despite the heinous comments and caricatures, the Obama family modeled a specifically Black feminine aesthetic with which many identified. Because Black women and girls historically are perceived as dangerous, loud, sex-crazed, and therefore not worthy of the opportunities they receive, the presentation of respectable and beautiful Black girls served as a public recognition and validation of Black women's assimilability into the highest echelons of American society.

While the caricatures and characterizations of the Obama parents centered on fabricated birtherism, radicalism, and likeness to racist ideologies, the Obama daughters were generally protected as young people while in the White House. Following the tradition of removing White House children from media hysterias following the Kennedys, the political and ideological place of the White House created a whitening effect on the Obama girls—they were essentially provided the protection of white kids because of this. The parenting skills of Michelle Obama were consistently referenced when discussing how the girls looked, dressed, or behaved at events. The Obama girls represented the possibilities for a future that materialized Rev. Dr. Martin Luther King Jr's oft-cited March on Washington speech, in which children manifested the hope of the Black community to be accepted and treated as citizens alongside their white peers. As the daughters of "the hope president" and the wishful materialization of King's speech, the Obama girls' characterizations harnessed ideals of hope, futurity, and prosperity for the US public and especially Black people. Unlike many Black girl peers who are positioned as always between innocence and guilt, girlhood and womanhood, Malia and Sasha represented a twenty-first-century Black future that celebrated them as virginal, hopeful, and beautiful—physical manifestations of the (Black) American Dream. The multiple layers of misrecognition, obscuring of Black girls' choices and desires, and privileging of others' beliefs about them structure the failure Malia and Sasha experience.

Separated from narratives of fast Black girls that circulated simultaneously while they occupied 1600 Pennsylvania Avenue, the

Obama girls provided an alternative vision of Black girlhood that encouraged others to both recognize their potential and see Black boys as the ones needing rescuing during the Obama years. Obama's 2014 national initiative, My Brother's Keeper, specifically aimed to address opportunities for Black boys because—as Salamishah Tillet contends—"our narrative of black dying is constructed as one of grieving mothers and sons gone too soon—a line that goes from Emmett to Trayvon. And while there is a grave truth to that lineage, it means that all children are not equally counted. It means this could not be the summer of Renisha McBride."[1] Their father's initiative cemented a crisis of Black boyhood and manhood, which visually matched the public outrage surrounding the murders of Trayvon Martin and Jordan Davis in 2012 and Michael Brown and Tamir Rice in 2014. If the murders of Black boys and men represented how much the US had not changed, the representations of beautiful and well-behaved Black women and girls in the White House articulated a successful American narrative of progress (confirmed with 2016 findings from the National Center for Education Statistics that showed Black women as the most educated population in the US). The Obama girls ideologically represented the best of Black integration and therefore lived generally unscathed in the public characterizations of their family during the Obama presidential years. However, the hopeful and respectful discussions about Malia and Sasha ended as the girls were firmly situated in their teenage years at the end of their father's presidency. Malia and Sasha were swiftly regarded as (potentially) fast Black girls, whose facial expressions and body language, hair and bodies, friendships and intimate interests became the evidence of deplorable parenting and character. Social media and their friend groups became evidence of their "wild" activities, representations to which their mother—the former Mom-in-Chief—still actively responds in public venues since the release of her memoir and documentary, *Becoming*, in 2018.

    Malia Obama was eighteen when videos and pictures of her living a typical teenage life began to flood the internet every few months. Particularly because her father, Barack Obama, was the first Black

US president from 2009 to 2017, Malia grew up as a public Black girl. Her mother, First Lady Michelle Obama, worked to keep her and her younger sister Sasha in school and away from paparazzi cameras; but as Black girls, Malia and Sasha were constantly surveilled. At the end of Obama's presidency, Malia began the process of deciding where to attend college. Following in her parents' footsteps, she began her college search at the Ivy League institutions of Princeton and Harvard. Alongside the narratives that the Obama public relations team circulated about how deeply Barack would be affected by Malia's matriculation—actively narrating him as a doting father—other news outlets tracked down Malia's friends' posts on social media. These posts—mostly from Snapchat—showed Malia at parties and having fun. The public became particularly enthralled with images of Malia dancing and smoking at Lallapalooza (an outdoor concert) in summer 2017, kissing an unidentified "man" in November 2017, and smoking again in November 2017.

The younger Obama daughter, Natasha (known publicly as Sasha), received similar treatment in the fall of 2018, when she began scoping out colleges to attend. Unlike her sister and parents, Sasha was interested in public universities like the one she chose, the University of Michigan. There were regular rumors about whether she would join a sorority, get a boyfriend as her older sister had, or participate in regular college activities. News outlets talked to other students to find out how Sasha was adjusting to college life, checking their stories against her parents' narration of dropping her off at college. Like Malia's images on Snapchat, Sasha's enjoyment of rap music on TikTok went viral, with many commenting on the differences between the two girls and how their public presentations mirrored one parent or the other. This surveillance and degradation of Malia and Sasha Obama bespeaks a larger cultural disdain for blackness and girlhood, especially available to the public eye.

The public fascination with these social media images, the constant conversation about the Obama girls and who they are becoming, and the comparisons between the girls and their parents illustrates a greater desire to surveil and control Black girls. Although they are the daughters of a past president, the public vilification of their parents, their parents' celebrity status, and the US cultural attitudes about Black girls (and social narratives about boy-crazed teen girls) circulate around Malia and Sasha as private citizens. Focusing on the cultural frenzy around Sasha and Malia Obama after their parents' exit from the White House, I explore how Black girls exist in a hypervisible space of surveillance and control. Turning their friends or classmates into reporters and their choices into indictments of their parents' (especially their mother's) ability to rear them, the Obama girls are subject to public concerns about their sexuality, their bodies (especially if they are pretty or not), and their futures. While articulated alongside the invisibility of Black women in the public sphere, the hypervisibility of Black girls is connected to age-old concerns about representations of blackness that are tied specifically to Black girls as future "race women" as well as racist concerns about Black girls' propensity for drugs, danger, and pregnancy.[2] By studying the Obama girls as the future of our collective investments in racial equality and economic prosperity in the US that surrounded their father, I frame the cultural fascination and subsequent horror assigned to these self-assured girls that defy cultural norms as a carceral extension of misogynoir in which a culture of surveillance is specifically honed on celebrity Black girls to determine their girliness, their blackness, and their sexualities. Ultimately, I find that despite these technologies, the Obama girls are instructive for how many Black girls learn how to navigate US surveillance cultures based in misogynoir.

Black Girls Online: Misogynoir and the Surveillance of Technology

From the racism of algorithms to the harassment of Black femmes online, our technological landscape precisely replicates the mistreatment of Black girls and women experienced daily. Internet scholar Safiya Noble uncovered the bias within Google search engines in her book *Algorithms of Oppression*; she explicates how capitalism undergirds the so-called colorblind ideologies of searches, presenting them as authoritative and objective, while obscuring the ways they inform and are constructed by people who input racist and sexist depictions of Black girls into the algorithmic coding.[3] It is not an accident that the social experiences of Black girls—in which they are treated as hypersexual, ugly, loud, and unwanted—match the ways that they are presented online despite their overwhelming use of platforms like Facebook/Instagram, Twitter, Snapchat, and TikTok. Beyond search technologies, Black girls are consistently perceived as knowledgeable about and always available for sexual activities. As Ebony Elizabeth Thomas reminds us, "The prevailing cultural script that has been handed down over the generations is that *some children are more innocent than others, and Black children are not innocent at all*. We notice this, but are not encouraged to voice it aloud, because the construction of childhood innocence on foundations of race is implied but never spoken, lest we offend others."[4] Therefore, the prevalence of Black girls like Sasha Obama online, especially in ways that connote excessiveness, always already communicates a womanishness that is sexually provocative and available for consumption. Ethnomusicologist Kyra Gaunt's work on Black girls' YouTube videos chronicles their digital sexualization since 2007; Gaunt argues that the "digital ecology" of social media like YouTube invites "context collapse" and "context collision" in which Black girls' bodies are "deprived of [their] locally-shared context and meaning though it is clearly registered in the practice of trolling, race-baiting, and slut-shaming."[5] Although Gaunt and I disagree on Black girls' knowledge of their self-presentation and understanding of other contexts that collide and collapse onto their twerking performances on platforms like YouTube, I concur that social media directs the technological gaze through which Black girls navigate their digital presence. I contend that digital platforms like YouTube or apps like Instagram, Snapchat, and TikTok invite surveillance, a technological collision of white supremacy's seductive racialized eroticism and beliefs in Black carcerality that mark Black bodies (especially feminized bodies) as in need of control.[6]

Dating back to the turn of the twentieth century, newly freed Black girls' and women's bodies were subject to the constant surveillance of their bodies and behavior through technology. Saidiya Hartman describes searching for young Black women in the archives of progressive reformers, people who had documented images of Black ghettos in northern cities; she explains, "The photographs coerced the black poor into visibility as a condition of policing and charity, making those bound to appear suffer the burden of representation ... extend[ing] an optic of visibility and surveillance that had its origins in slavery and the administered logic of the plantation. (To be visible was to be target for uplift or punishment, confinement or violence)."[7] Hartman clearly identifies how photographs of Black girls and women were used as evidence of Black depravity, using technology to target the bodies and living spaces in need of rehabilitation. Aimee Meredith Cox confirms the continued placement of social, economic, and political anxieties onto Black girls' bodies in the 2000s in *Shapeshifters*. Cox notes that the Jezebel stereotype does not apply to Black girls in the same way as Black women such that "Black girls can be fast or promiscuous, but their youth or minor status requires that the state be accountable for their behavior to some degree, which usually translates to the surveillance and disciplining of their bodies and sexual expression. Yet state policing of the intimate and sexual lives of Black girls may look no different from the same policing of the lives of Black women."[8] Together, Hartman and Cox explicate the historical and contemporary cultures of surveillance that Black girls experience, whether they color inside the lines of respectability or decidedly choose different modes of being. Because of race, gender, and age, Black girls are subject to surveillance cultures that use their parents, friends, and technology to police acceptable and unacceptable agency, autonomy, and sexual expression.[9]

An advancement of technology and social media connectivity, TikTok videos provide the ocular opportunity to police Black girls as they display their intimate lives for (their own) entertainment. While Black girls have used TikTok as well as other platforms to communicate their innovation, laughter, dance skills, political affiliations, or a myriad of other things, the histories of Black girls online predicate their sexualization by others.[10] Others use Black girls' social media performances and commentaries as indictments of their social ratchetness and sexual promiscuity; social media "challenges"—which I understand as campaigns by one user (usually a high-profile influencer or celebrity) for others to replicate a dance or song in their own creative way—of the late 2010s and early 2020s presented the opportunity for folks to judge Black girls' bodies, especially in the cases of the #silhouettechallenge and the #bussitchallenge. Both challenges required that users turned the camera on themselves, either displaying their silhouettes while dancing to sexually suggestive music or transitioning from pajamas to party clothes while booty-popping to newcomer rapper Erica Banks's song "Buss It."

Beyond social media spaces created by and with Black girls, the media is also complicit in using technology to popularize ideas about which girls are worthy of being noticed and the use of technology as surveillance. Media narratives that construct US and foreign white girls as ideal citizens worthy of attention and affection contrastingly construct Black girls and other girls of color in the US and elsewhere as consistently at-risk, poor, and in need of government control due to violence or local so-called backward practices.[11] Media scholar Sarah Projansky argues that within the contemporary mediascape, there is a "cultural obsession" with girls that is based on the convergence of celebrity culture, girl power rhetoric, and neoliberalism; she contends, "Media incessantly look at and invite us to look at girls. Girls are objects at which we gaze, whether we want to or not.... Media turn girls into spectacles—visual objects on display" that are either "fabulous" or "scandals."[12] In this way, all girls are subject to the spectacularization—literally being made into messy or mesmerizing objects—for public entertainment. However, Black girls—via the cultural histories of racism and rhetorics of control in a postplantation world—are always scandalous, even as they exist in fabulous circumstances. The rise of social media platforms like

TikTok, Snapchat, and Instagram invite a hyperocular opportunity—we can be on high alert at all times for any ounce of "real life" from celebrities, and if we miss it, the news media ensures that the public is informed about the births, marriages, deaths, and general social media posts of celebrities (so much so that TMZ stories have gone from tabloid to breaking news in just fifteen years). We can even set alarms and notifications so that we are the first to know when new information is shared. For Black people, and women especially, (social) media audiences can witness everything from our deaths at the hands of police officers and vigilantes to the abundant wealth of our businesses and bodies.

The convergence of social media technologies, algorithmic bias, and phone-based cameras has invited a synoptic premediated authenticity. By "synoptic premediated authenticity," I mean that many users on social media platforms—especially celebrities of color—are able to interact with and follow the few so-called important people, and these few are said to be their authentic selves when they post about their personal lives, performances, and respond to others, although their posts are preapproved and curated through the use of marketing professionals and social media managers.[13] The ability to see famous people as they eat at restaurants, talk to or text their celebrity friends, read stories to their children, conduct rehearsals for upcoming performances, make choices on makeup, hair, and wardrobe, and interact with fans has produced a proximity to their lived experience that makes users believe they are able to engage an authentic self beyond the professional persona. This process of mimesis, which I discuss in *Buy Black: How Black Women Transformed US Pop Culture* (2022) in the case of Nicki Minaj, is exacerbated for Black women.[14] Even when celebrities acknowledge and show the falsification of their personal reality shows via social media, the media considers these performances that much more authentic.[15]

Therefore, in the case of Black girls like the Obama girls, the confluence of perceived social media realness, carceral surveillance of blackness and female-identified people, obsession with girls and their sexual choices, and perceptions of "Black cool" encourages the media to use whatever means necessary to learn about their friends and their whereabouts; this process in turn encourages audiences (fans and haters alike) to comment on, judge, and speculate about Black girls' and women's choices.[16] This optic-informed speculation not only harms Black women and girls due to the privileging of racist and sexist beliefs about them, but it also produces the conditions through which they must create and understand their agentive selves.

City Girl Sasha: The Making of Ratchet Black Girlhood

Because the Obama girls are also treated as public figures, due to their father's presidency and mother's subsequent celebrity, their public presentation has been constructed by themselves, their parents, and the media through narratives about who they are (and are not) which are supported by the surveillance that collates information about them from social media and others around them. Through their father's interviews and books, their mother's books, documentary, and podcast, as well as their friends' social media and classmates' observations, Malia and Sasha are constantly of conversation even as they actively try to live private lives. The subsequent surveillance of the Obama girls mirrors similar attempts to control and scrutinize Black girls in educational settings that Black girlhood scholars such as Ruth Nicole Brown, Monique Morris, Venus Evans-Winters, Nikki Jones, and others have identified. This surveillance also reflects concerns about the carceral uses of technology on Black girls and other minoritized people in digital and everyday spaces that scholars Safiya Noble, Kyra Gaunt, Kishonna Gray, Savannah Shange, and others have theorized. Both the scrutiny and social media surveillance coalesce as the public narrative about the Obama girls' own self-presentation as Black girls. Particularly through their appearances in their friends' social media posts, Malia and Sasha are subject to context collapse, in which "each view (also known as an impression) of a black girl . . . [is] a cipher for creating the discourse of racial and gender ideology, as well as for the actual exchange of commerce as social capital in the attention economy surrounding rap and popular music videos."[17] While Gaunt argues that we must teach Black girls' media literacy so they understand the implications for the types of content their upload online, the Obama girls are well aware of the misogynoir that encourages others to analyze every aspect of their bodies, their friends, and their expressions.

In December 2020, a TikTok video surfaced of Sasha and five friends performing a choreographed dance to Popp Hunna's song "Adderall (Corvette Corvette)" (as was typical of TikTok videos at the time). Although the video was posted by one of Sasha's friends, her placement in the middle and the subsequent circulation of the video on other social media sites and in the news presented the video as her own. In commentary about the video, many Twitter users commented about her beauty, her nails, her necklace, her hair, and the presence (or lack thereof) of other Black people in her friend group. As the only Black girl in the video, Sasha's presence heightened conversations about Black girls' friend groups and whether there was enough influence of Black people in her social circle. While many adored her presence reflecting on how she had "come into her own," others questioned where her other Black friends were, why her and her friends were together during a global pandemic that encouraged people to only congregate with people of their household, and why her parents would allow this public presentation of her. Some questioned her song choice because she mouthed the lyric "bitch" as she danced; their outrage over the lyric mirrored their concern over a TikTok video in which she mouthed "fuck" following the lyrics of City Girl rapper JT's verse in the song "Said Sum" in October 2020. Once a photo of her surfaced in a crop top in late December 2020, Twitter users dubbed her "City Girl Sasha."

While hip-hop feminists would herald Sasha Obama's new moniker as an example of contemporary feminist formations that allow Black girls and women to embrace the fullness of their humanity, including their sexuality, the adjective "city girl" bespeaks a public performance of sexuality like the rap group, City Girls. Known for their sexually explicit lyrics in songs like "Pussy Talk" and "Twerk" that celebrate Black women's sexual agency and rejection of respectability, City Girls duo JT and Yung Miami represent a new crop of Black women rappers who embrace their sexual allure and prowess as what hip-hop feminist Kyra March claims as "percussive feminism."[18] March argues that City Girls are within a cultural genealogy of Black women rappers whose feminism is "loud as fuck," "dynamic," "bold and goes against all tradition."[19] They are and represent Black women who choose a highly sexualized public representation even as they recognize and know intimately the ideologies that construct Black women as ugly Jezebels in need of control.

Artists like City Girls, Megan Thee Stallion, Cardi B, and others have created phrases to demarcate their fan bases (City Girls, Hotties, and Bardigang respectively), yet we have no evidence that Sasha Obama identifies with any of these groups. Because others have imposed the name onto her semipublic TikTok performances in mostly celebratory ways, "City Girl Sasha" connotes a particular racialized and highly gendered sartorial-sexual politics in line with Black and hip-hop feminist theorizing that claims power and freedom for Black girls and women that perform "ratchet feminism." In other words, "City Girl Sasha," claims a fluency in hip-hop culture, Black womanhood, and the sexualized bodily presentation of Black women in contemporary US social media culture based on several TikTok videos (none of which are longer than sixty seconds).

Described by hip-hop education scholar Ashley Payne as a dismissal of "the oppressiveness of respectability," ratchetness serves as a cloak on all things related to Black women who are loud, outspoken, expressive, or promiscuous.[20] Sasha Obama's so-called ratchet aesthetic—a pejorative label for the visual abundance that her long white nails, eyelashes, long hair (possibly weaved extensions), and performance of sexually explicit lyrics offer—then communicates her own dismissal of middle-class respectability for which her mother, Michelle Obama, has become the Black cultural patron saint. As Payne puts it, "Cardi B has become an anti-respectability icon" due to her "carefree demeanor coupled with her long nails, loud and outspoken voice, sexually provocative clothing, and open discussion and presentation of her sexuality" with which City Girls (via their collaboration with Cardi on the song "Twerk"), and now Sasha Obama, are also associated.[21]

While others identify Obama's recorded, uploaded, scandalized, and swiftly removed fifteen-second TikTok videos as evidence of childrearing gone awry or a snippet of her true self captured for the world to see, Sasha Obama's performances harness the narratives her parents and others create of her. Through her brief articulations of subjectivity in TikTok videos and knowledge of how others use surveillance technologies, Sasha Obama performs an allegiance to the "aesthetics of excess" rather than any self-proclaimed ratchetness (especially as her life is staunchly middle class). Jillian Hernandez explicates that to "present aesthetic excess is to make oneself hypervisible," using "the body creatively, admir[ing] one's self-image."[22] In this way, we see Sasha Obama perform "sexual-aesthetic excess," a concept Hernandez uses to identify the racializing discourse that mark working-class Black and Latinx bodily "dress and comportment" as "'too much': too sexy, too ethnic, too young, too cheap, too loud."[23]

Twenty-first-century Black cultural politics contextualize Sasha Obama's performances as a subjective expression because of the mimesis that occurs on social media platforms. However, as a private citizen who is surveilled like a popular public figure, Obama recognizes her ability to direct social commentary and ire. As a Black girl, especially one that is on the social line between girl and woman, Obama knows intimately the ways that her body will be read on social media platforms and how those platforms inform and impact conversations about Black girls (ratchet or otherwise) in everyday life. As a Black girl (and a college student) who is constantly part of public discussion, used to praise or demonize her parents, Sasha Obama is hyperaware and actively uses the aesthetics, politics, and algorithmic logics of social media to create a public persona that I believe she eventually will convert into monetary gain.

Like Mother, Like Daughter: Constructing Sasha Obama

While much of Sasha Obama's public life until college was overcast by news stories about her father and mother, their family dynamic became a great source of curiosity and pride. Via her mother's "Mom-in-Chief" performances of Black motherhood, the public became privy to tidbits of information about Sasha and who she was becoming as the Obama family's time in the White House came to an end. In particular, Sasha Obama's personality became a point of concern (as had her mother's previously and since) after the 2016 State Dinner. Covered in the media as a type of coming out for the Obama children, the final State Dinner of the Obama administration was the first for the Obama girls at age seventeen (Malia) and fourteen (Sasha). News media covered how President Obama got teary eyed describing his oldest daughter's impending college departure (Malia's response was an eye roll) and how Sasha Obama excitedly chatted with Ryan Reynolds. This first public presentation of Malia and Sasha started the post-Obama speculation about who the girls would be, including discussions of their beauty, their sexual choices, and what their futures will hold.

In their December 2016 interview with People+ magazine, Barack and Michelle Obama reflect on their time in the White House. Michelle Obama speaks about how they hoped to exude a moral standard for all kids by creating programming in and around the White House that would encourage children to feel connected to the first Black family, using their daughters' own interests and desires as a benchmark for other children. They discussed too how shifts in American culture during their administration is being and will be carried forward by their daughters, Sasha and Malia. Rhetorically, the Obamas repeatedly communicate their hope in what their children will do, who their children are as "smart, good people," and that Sasha always seems first in their public commentary about their children.[24] Perhaps it is a slight of tongue, but it's not random that "Sasha and Malia" is the exact phrasing we know and use to discuss the Obama girls—so much so that it seems abnormal to say,

"Malia and Sasha." Although Malia is older, Sasha is always uttered first. Since the 2016 interview, Michelle Obama released the bestselling memoir of all time, *Becoming*, and continues to speak about her daughters (and she is constantly asked about them via media's obsession with girls), their influence, and who they are becoming as women. When asked by Oprah Winfrey what is the best advice Obama has given her daughters or a running theme of their childhood, she says that "they have to walk their own walk. They cannot define themselves by looking at each other. . . . Give themselves a moment to figure out who they want to be in the world."[25] Obama explains that she does not follow her daughters' social media pages, but notes that "they are being watched" by older cousins and family friends. This admission illustrates not only the structure of twenty-first-century parenting, but more so explains the pressures that Malia and Sasha experience.

While their mother may communicate that they should learn themselves, build a life based on their own terms, and not center other people's opinions of them, they know as well as she does that others are watching. Sasha, known for being extroverted and "scary" like her mother, has been raised to know the optics surrounding her public presentation from a young age. With her mother's consistent reminders to "walk your walk" and the steady hand of their maternal grandmother in their lives in Chicago and in the White House, Sasha knows how Black women are perceived and the space available to them in the US public sphere. Sasha Obama is aware of what options she has as the daughter of the former president and first lady.

And yet, anthropologist and choreographer Aimee Meredith Cox reminds us, "questions of sex and sexuality for young Black women are not simply matters of desire, survival sex, victimization, or morality. These young women consciously try to figure out how they would like to experience sex as pleasure, as part of a loving healthy relationship, and as a form of self-expression."[26] As evidenced by her performances and their swift removal on social media, Sasha like other contemporary Black girls and women are invested in hip-hop because of the possibilities for expressive, including sexual, agency. As southern hip-hop scholar Regina Bradley brilliantly explains, "Southern black girlhood is unique in that is a navigation of how to 'carry myself' as a lady—often the crux of any type of respectability for black women—while situating myself in a sociocultural moment where being ladylike or quiet or politically correct does not mean everything will be all right."[27] Although Sasha and Malia were not raised in the South, their grandmother's and mother's attention to how they carry themselves while knowing themselves outside who the world constructs them to be is the same type of navigation Bradley names within her own experience. Black girls and women across the diaspora, but especially in the United States, know well the stereotypes that are thrown at us for simply existing; intimately, we know the hurt caused from being called "everything but a child of God" (as the Black Church saying goes). And we know this because of the intergenerational conversations we have in our homes, in hair salons, in churches, and in civic organization meetings—we learn very quickly and usually through nonverbal "community intelligence" which ways we should represent ourselves to lessen any scorn or judgment.[28] But as Bradley mentions, and we know too, a moment does not exist in which Black girls and women could be ladylike and "everything will be all right." There is always judgment. But we exist anyway, and hip-hop allows space for us to both shake our booties the way we like and critique the misogynoir we experience from all corners of the world; we celebrate the unique beauty and potentialities of our best friends as they dance and laugh and explore the world through hip-hop, even as we recognize how the rhetoric of bitches and hos gets used against us. Sasha knows this too and uses hip-hop in the same ways we do.

The Failures of Obama's Promise

Since the Obamas left the White House in January 2017, the political media has turned to a new presidential family and discussion. But the fascination with the children of the Obama family has seemingly continued in other media—with a growing intensity as social media has gone from a digital extracurricular activity to a mainstay of American culture. While Malia's collegiate journey began as her family's presidential journey ended, the media and those around her took an active interest in using her and her behaviors as some indication of who the Obamas had been the whole time. They posted photos and encouraged discussions of her hair, her body, and her relationships as she went about normal teenage activities. Folks were concerned that her smoking or kissing a white boy communicated some nefarious household behaviors; for many, Black girls do not display affection, make "poor choices," or display their bodies in public. Therefore, Malia's public presentation where she was, in many ways, a "normal" child was particularly salacious to discuss. Despite how they were treated from 2008 to 2017, Malia and the Obama family, arguably, did not yet know how the public would treat them after leaving the White House—as Michelle Obama puts it, "We lived in a bubble"—but they learned swiftly that social media and the public obsession with them and their girls would create narratives about who they are, how they were raised, and who they would become beyond their White House years.

In the years since Malia's public bashing though, the Obamas have gotten smarter about their public presence and have actively worked to create narratives about each other for the public to consume. Michelle Obama's *Becoming* and *The Light We Carry* books, thirty-four-city publicity tours, and podcast (as well as the other Netflix deals and media interviews in which she and her husband have participated) spurred public conversations about the Obamas' lives within and beyond the White House. The Obama parents—through funny jokes and seemingly off-the-cuff anecdotes—have constructed personas about their daughters.

For example, in a July 2019 *British Vogue* interview with the Duchess of Sussex Megan Markle (she guest edited the September issue in which the interview is printed), Michelle Obama describes how motherhood has made her realize how different her daughters'—this time Malia and Sasha—personalities are from one another. She says, "In some ways, Malia and Sasha couldn't be more different. One speaks freely and often; one opens up on her own terms. One shares her innermost feelings, the other is content to let you figure it out. Neither approach is better or worse, because they've both grown into smart, compassionate and independent young women, fully capable of paving their own paths."[29] While Mrs. Obama does not say which daughter expresses herself in which way, Barack Obama describes his daughters' personalities similarly in an interview with David Letterman in January 2018—just a year after leaving office. He describes Malia as forthcoming and interested in feedback—like Mrs. Obama's "one shares her innermost feelings"—while Sasha is less forthcoming and is fine with "letting you figure it out" as Mrs. Obama puts it later.

The two interviews together—from January 2018 and September 2019—in some ways craft public narratives of Malia and Sasha that reflect how the public should see and understand them; after Malia's public interactions, there have been few sightings of her unlike her early college days. Sasha, on the other hand, has made use of public obsessions with her through other people's social media posts. While it is reported that she does not have a personal profile on TikTok, Snapchat, or other platforms, Sasha has been the trending topic three times in 2020. The posts, usually short and taken down within minutes, illustrate a Black girl enjoying herself, her friends, and her newfound freedom at nineteen. Despite all the ways others have tried to construct her public persona (and how Sasha knows they will respond), she shows up anyway.

Like other Black girls who know and exist in the cloud of public critique with whatever they do—namely, Megan Thee Stallion, Lori Harvey, and Jordyn Woods who all became major topics of conversation regarding their sexual choices and their bodies in 2019 and 2020—Sasha and Malia have learned how to best express themselves as others maintain an obsession about who they are and what they do. Malia even became a writer on a satirical horror Amazon Prime Video series, *Swarm*, in 2023; the show starring Dominique Fishback follows celebrity obsession, mental health, and the invisibility of Black girls. While hypervisibility for Black girls will not disappear due to misogynoir and the machine of social media likes and clicks, Malia and Sasha Obama show that they have learned as many Black girls do—my body is my own, and I will create the life I want regardless of what is said about me.

Black patriarchal dominance and surveillance subject Black girls to the idea that their bodies are not their own, and they are not able to claim agency without being called "fast." The next chapter explains how Black girls regulate their own and others' opinions through self-assuredness, dictating how others should treat them. Even in the face of the threat of violence, Black girls determine the possibilities of their worlds.

CHAPTER 3

Loving Fast-Tailed Girls

Queen Sugar, Southern Black Girlhood, and Theological Abuse

> Folks don't like nobody being too proud or too free.
> She's [Shug Avery] no more than a jook-joint jezebel.
> —The Color Purple (1985 film)

> I took it to mean what my cousin once meant—black girlhood ends whenever a man says it ends. Two sides to every story. Almost ready. She a ho. Those are the kind of comments I have heard hundreds, if not thousands, of times, from men and women, to excuse violence against black women and girls. If one is "ready" for what a man wants from her, then by merely existing she has consented to his treatment of her. Puberty becomes permission.
> —Tressie McMillan Cottom, *Thick*

Described as "almost ready," "ho," or "fast," Black girls learn that childhood innocence has not been afforded them and that their perceived sexual knowledge becomes the basis for the ways that boys and men, women and other girls, demarcate the girls that are disposable and the girls that are worthy of protection. Black girls are rarely in the latter group because they are consistently subject to adultification, the belief that they are already as knowledgeable as adults and should be treated as adults.[1] Even at home, Black girls learn that their safety and protection is second to their proximity to being fast and the desires of men. They learn early that being considered fast is a matter of social construction, how others including those they love see them, rather than any factual evidence or knowledgeable attribution. They learn that the people they love and the places they live are not and will not be places of sanctuary because, as sociologist Tressie McMillan Cottom states, "home is where they love you until you're a ho."[2] Robbed of childhood innocence, physical and emotional safety, and protection from sexual trauma, Black girls are consistently failed by those closest to them—Black men and women who facilitate girls' sexual trauma in the most intimate and familial spaces, threaded by religious doctrine and misogynoir.

Denotative definitions of "fast" describe someone who is quick to learn, acquire, or accomplish something, someone who has early exposure to an idea or concept. Therefore, when used to describe Black girls in a colloquial sense, fast puts the onus on Black girls as individuals who are invested in being too quick to learn or acquire sexual experiences or have been intentional in early exposure to their own sexual pleasures; in this sense, a fast Black girl is one that learns things about her body and sexual intimacies earlier than the norm for other girls (usually white) and boys (usually Black). Regardless of the discursive inaccuracies of "fast" being applied to the sexual desires of children, the perception of Black girls across the globe follows this colloquial definition in which they are believed to be prematurely ready to participate in sexual acts.[3] Before the forming of breasts or the first loosening of walls along the uterus even, others determine some girls to be fast simply through the ways that they exist. Whether in the US and Canada, or in Caribbean, European, and African countries, Black girls are believed to be hypersexual, especially when they exhibit self-determination and confidence in themselves.

A "fast-tailed girl" is "a black girl with confidence who speaks up for herself, wants to express her femininity visually, has a normal interest in boys, gets unwanted attention from adult men, and/or has male friends."[4] While writer and photographer Trudy's definition includes "tailed" as a specific harkening to the buttocks of Black girls, naturally recalling the Western obsession with Black booties, a Black girl's developing body or her attitude can be hailed as fast. Despite the varying degrees of interest in sexual experiences, Black girls who simply open their mouths in ways that others do not like are believed to be fast and therefore deserving of any and all sexual harassment, violence, or abuse that befalls them; said differently, Black girls who speak up at all are considered fast whether or not their bodies have experienced hormonal changes. As I argue elsewhere, Black girls learn to develop feistiness amidst a world that is violent toward them by emulating the ways that their mothers, aunts, and other community members interact with the world.[5] Despite this emulation, Black girls, both real and fictional, are perceived as always already behaving beyond their social position or older than their birth date would determine.

While Black girls' reputations foreground sexual prowess alongside self-possession, many characterizations overwhelmingly emanate from non-Black women and girl cultural producers. Therefore, this chapter examines the visual representations of Black girls created and produced by Black women to consider the representational politics of Black girls that are interpreted as fast. I consider what role Black women's images have in discourse that allows for the abuse of Black girls by family and strangers in their lives. Perhaps we can fail less by shifting our collective responses to Black girls who seem self-assured on screen and in the everyday.

To map "fast-tailed girl" discourse, I consider representations of Black girls in the critically acclaimed Oprah Winfrey Network show *Queen Sugar*. Adapted loosely from a novel of the same name, *Queen Sugar* was created, written, and executive produced by Ava DuVernay and Oprah Winfrey—both Black women actively shaping contemporary Black representation in media. DuVernay captures the beauty and sensuality in southern Black contexts in many ways, particularly in the display of love between siblings, between mother and child, between partners in business, between land and people, and between lovers. Through a consideration of the *Queen Sugar* character, Keke, in digital discourse, I explore the social construction of Black girlhood in the US as it pertains to "fastness" and where the sexual promiscuity narrative shapes how Black girls are seen in popular culture overall. Juxtaposed with how audiences responded to DuVernay's self-assured Black girl characters like Keke on social media, and the purposeful and communal demonization of so-called fast Black girls in everyday life across US geographical spaces, I found that DuVernay provides an alternate reading of (dark-skinned, southern, self-possessed) bold Black girls that encourages our responses to be grounded in how Black girls live. Said differently, I examine how DuVernay's character challenges discourses of fast Black girls situated within the cultural and geospatial politics of blackness, youth, sexuality, and cultural misogynoir.[6]

A drama based in rural Louisiana, *Queen Sugar* follows the Bordelon siblings—the journalist-activist Nova living in New Orleans, the businesswoman and wife-manager of a professional athlete Charley living in Los Angeles, and a formerly incarcerated father Ralph Angel still living on their father's farm—as they navigate the aftermath of their father's death. Although their father's sugarcane farm was betrothed to all of them, Nova, Charley, and Ralph Angel have differing ideas about how to respect their father's legacy as they create the lives they wish to lead under the watchful guidance of their father's sister, Violet. While Nova is childfree, she alongside her siblings and "Aunt Vi" work to create a healthy and loving family environment for Charley's fifteen-year-old son, Micah, and Ralph Angel's young son, Blue, as well as maintain their father's strong standing in the Black community of St. Josephine. The Bordelon family is consistently met with contradictions in gendered perceptions of their lives, racist terror from the ever-present carceral system, and the afterlives of slavery and contract labor from the white Landry/Boudreaux family that has majority stake in all sugarcane land and processing. Despite their struggles and disagreements, *Queen Sugar* unfolds the mundanity and brilliance of southern Black life, the histories that complicate their everyday experiences, and the futures they wish to manifest through love and loss.

One of the most captivating instances of a budding romance in season 1 of the television drama is between Charley's son, Micah, and family friend, Keke. We are first introduced to Keke (Tanyell Waivers) in season 1, episode 9, after a hurricane leaves the Bordelon family to clear out tree limbs from Aunt Vi's yard; Keke and her stepfather Boogie stop by to help them. In their first interaction, Micah (Nicholas Ashe) shyly eyes Keke with a grin on his face, while she jokes about him "catching a heat stroke" with the temperature change in St. Jo and how much taller he looks in his Instagram photos.[7] Despite her seemingly steady gaze and speech, her body language shifts to a performed maturity; from an easy arms-hanging stance, she moves her hands into her pockets and then shifts again to her left hand on her hip. This movement along with her culturally apropos dozens-playing illustrates her interest, even while she is unsure of this Californian newcomer.

Later in the episode, Keke approaches Micah about more posts on his Instagram and playfully laughs about his response to shotgun sounds during "deer season." Before leaving for the day, Keke asks Micah about surfing as a way to ask about his relationship status: "Do you surf? Surf camp in Malibu? So, you got yourself a Malibu girlfriend, too?"[8] While she does not shy away from asking questions that she wants answers to, Keke's interest in Micah is illustrated by trying to get him to talk about himself. Micah was a bit shy initially, but he too follows up on his interest and follows her to the car when she gets called to leave: "It was really cool hanging out with you." Keke makes it clear that Micah must initiate interactions between them beyond their interactions today: "You won't see me . . . unless you want to." While Micah laughs and is unsure of how to proceed, they look at each other in the eyes steadily. Keke offers, "Follow me on IG" (a shorthand for Instagram) and provides her handle.[9] Both of their full toothy grins follow, as Keke makes her way to the truck, and it pulls off.

After only this brief interaction between the two characters, audiences took to social media to address this budding love. Marking her as "fast" and "aggressive," Twitter fingers worked to remake Keke's opinionated, self-confidence as the beginnings of an unchecked Jezebel; on November 16, 2016, @CatwalkDarling, for example, comments after Keke's ride pulls off from the scene: "This fast ass little girl on Queen Sugar is something else. And Micah ain't ready for that

LOVING FAST-TAILED GIRLS

type of sass." Swift to remake Keke as a sassy and fast girl, much too advanced for Micah, users like @CatwalkDarling positioned Keke as the aggressor and as a teenage girl that already knew too much, too quickly. Evidenced only by Keke's straightforward candor, the Jezebel discourse easily flung at Black women encircled Keke's fictionalized portrayal of Black girlhood. While K. Sue Jewell characterizes a Jezebel as a "fair-complexioned African American female" who "reinforces cultural stereotypes regarding the hypersexuality of the African American female, who yearns for sexual encounters," Keke's desire to determine her own romantic relationships as a (fictional) dark-complected African American girl in the South led some social media users to construct her speech, her body, and her confidence as worthy of disrespect.[10]

Black feminist scholars such as Patricia Hill Collins and many others have theorized the multifaceted ways that Black women are constructed in US media and culture. However, it is equally important to understand the construction of Black girls' as distinct from those of Black women. As a growing number of scholars dedicated to the experiences of Black girls in the US have argued, it is important to create a theory of Black girlhood that does not presuppose or derive itself from Black womanhood.[11] In *The Black Girlhood Studies Collection* (2019), I cite "historical knowledge, cultural attitudes, and cultural rhetoric" as the reasons why the theorizing of Black girls has stayed tightly linked to that of Black women.[12] Important for the discussion here, I contend that intraracial cultural attitudes encouraged Black women and girls to promote and adhere to respectability and adultification to prove themselves worthy of respect. Specifically for Black girls, I write,

> In this logic, being worthy of respect through our actions would save us from those who sought to do us harm; respectability would save us. Much like our historical knowledge of Black girls in past times, we crafted adult attitudes and habits for the sake of protection. This protection, however, cost many of us knowledge of self and of joy. We worked harder to

be worthy of dignity and respect and lost some of ourselves along the way.[13]

The threat of being perceived as fast by women and men in their lives encouraged Black girls to draw a line at knowledge of self, imposing their attention to others' perceptions of them, and in many ways has allowed the proliferation of misogynoir as well as justifications for abuse that center Black girls as the accusers rather than those they have accused. I extend these discussions and the charge to create theories of and methodologies for studying Black girlhood that focus on Black girls' self-knowledge by expanding from Keke's characterization in *Queen Sugar* and on Twitter to theorize Black girls' experiences in relationship to the misogynoir they experience.

The Subtlety of Southern Black Girlhood

Over the course of my formative years in Durham, NC, I struggled with how little Black girls like me (and Latina and Indigenous girls like the ones I befriended in college) knew about sex and sexuality growing up. In conversations about adolescent sex education, I was struck by the lack of information in schools and in our families about our bodies, by the oversimplification of explanations about consent, and by the negative attitudes toward sex, sexuality, and pregnancy when it comes to girls of color. This lack of information, for some reason, seemed to coincide with ideas of girls like me being loose or fast, which distinguished us and which constructed our experiences with men and women in sexual relationships as we aged. "Fast" in particular was used as a marker of sexual depravity, always in reference to a girl who had breasts, hips, and a butt "like a woman." As a performatively "good clean Christian Black girl" in the South, I was constantly inundated with ideas of what kind of girl/woman I should strive not to be. Yet, I encountered very few conversations about what experiences of sex or sexuality were available if us good girls walked the straight and narrow path of respectability. Pleasure-centered discourses around sex and sexuality, especially for women and girls, were completely absent; where, if anywhere, I wondered, are experiences of sex and sexuality appropriate, possible, and even pleasurable?

Black girls in the South are regularly punished for questions or ideas around sexuality. Based in heteropatriarchal readings of religious books, sexual scripts confine southern Black girls' body autonomy and sexual agency because of the false correlation between sexuality and sin.[14] These narratives structure not only the ways that Black girls interact with peers their own age around sex and sexuality but also how older people construct identities of Black girls specifically as fast or loose. The sexual scripts Black girls receive collapse sexual exploration under eighteen and outside of marriage with punitive responses from friends, family, and a masculine-gendered deity. Their age allows for punishment via rebuke and shame, while their older sisters, mothers, and aunts are surveilled for their sexual agency and childfree choices; Black girl sexual scripts serve to chastise Black girls and women and compare their behaviors to those of (non-Black) other women. Cultural theorist Brittney Cooper cites her grandmother's theology—"A theology of grown Black women, was one predicated on dissent from a set of biblical truths and social mores that shamed women, cast female sexuality as bad, dirty, and evil, and suggested that marriage was the only proper context through which women could express their sexual selves"—as a way to understand how fastness was used against Black women and girls.[15] And yet, Cooper's grandmother perhaps like my own still circulated ideas about girls' lack of chastity based on the same biblical rules they rejected as adults.

These biblically based sexual scripts aim to maintain "white patriarchal hegemony" through the "stereotypes and false images surrounding Black female sexuality [that] provide the foundation for sexual exploitation and humiliation."[16] White patriarchal hegemony has been circulated and maintained through the misuse and false interpretation of biblical stories, constantly forcing all girls and women to juxtapose themselves against characters like Eve, Naomi, and the unnamed Samaritan woman at the well. For women generally, the construction of our foremother, Eve, as licentious and predetermined to be the downfall of man always already constructs us as stumbling blocks in paths to (men's and our own) holiness; this is expanded exponentially for Black women as they are characterized as lewd and conniving like the biblical character, Ahab, and how the downfall of the kingdom was attributed to her sexuality in 1 Kings 16–22.[17] Black women's treatment, as always already fallen and able to destroy men, families, kingdoms, worlds, and even the theological construction of men as perfect until women seduce them, is the basis for all interactions of white power with Black bodies, and these ideas "have been so insidious that they continue to influence Black people's responses to sexual issues."[18] Black southern girls are raised within theological genealogies that privilege these sexual scripts, which in turn determine our bodies, our knowledge, and our experiences as licentious on the very basis of being girls and Black.

Religion scholar Tamura Lomax in *Jezebel Unhinged* (2018) bridges the personal and theological explanations Cottom, Cooper, Durham, and Douglas theorize into a discourse of "ho theology" that includes popular culture and how the Black Church and its cultural referents uphold Black patriarchy, the nuclear family, and the false dichotomy between good and bad women—or as I heard it ad nauseam in Sunday school and women's conferences: the "Proverbs 31 woman" and the "Jezebel." I include a lengthy quote of Lomax because she fully illustrates how Black girls and women encounter the "fast" characterizations of themselves. Lomax brilliantly explains how Jezebel is a trope that

> Even as she may be appropriated individually, she is simultaneously always already historically created from without. She is the white man's oeuvre and as old as North American black women's and girls' ungraspable purity and intoxicating subjectivity. But she is also biblical Jezebel remixed, revived, and incarnate—Black Church version. She is the stranglehold that shaped the lustful eyes of the church elder during my youth.

She is the veteran gaze of the black women street preacher who called my college friends and I jezebel sluts every time we walked from the train station to the bus stop in downtown Atlanta, Georgia. She is the imagined self that many black Christian women summon when singing and praying, "Wash me clean, oh Lord!" And she is the muse in contemporary black religious and cultural productions, where we encounter not only jezebel but her spawn: the ho—black folk's thot, white folks' whore.[19]

Southern Black girls and women like Lomax, Cottom, Cooper, Durham, and me experienced the construction of good versus evil/fast/ho/Jezebel at home, in everyday interactions with other Black women and men, in television shows and at community events. The trope of an evil, loose, and therefore impure woman manifests in every single aspect of southern Black girls' and women's lives, structuring how we understand our bodies, our desires, our holiness (or lack thereof), and our standing in our communities.

However, research on the construction of good girls and fast girls has focused mostly on white girls and the use of slut in their sexual experiences, completely erasing the ways that slut (or ho, or the scarlet letter, or fast) are racialized misogynist statements of the same ilk. For example, reading Emily White's *Fast Girls*, Lorraine Kenny's *Daughters of Suburbia*, or Leora Tanenbaum's *Slut!* on the experiences of hypersexualized girls makes it clear that scholarly discussions of "the slut" never considered the ways that the terminology exists in communities of color. From interviews with over 150 girls and women after she asks for contributors to an article on slut culture, White writes, "over time I realized the stories sounded so similar in part because the America they were originating from was the same: small-town or suburban white America. Most of the girls who contacted me were rooted in this demographic; the slut story was not something that seemed to have an urban or multiracial backdrop."[20] And yet, White's narrative begins with how a half-white, half-Filipina girl was treated in her high school; while she clearly notes that ethnic/racial difference of her childhood classmate, White is quick to dismiss racial antagonisms in "multicultural" settings as an underlying factor. The markers of difference she names, however, illustrate the ways that narratives of girlhood constrict and contour for girls of color. In this way, race, breast and hip development before other girls, differences in socioeconomic status from others, personality (in other words, "they were not afraid of cussing someone out"), and geography play a huge role in the ways that girls are perceived as hypersexual beings.[21] Whether called slut/whore/hoe (or ho), fast/loose/fast-tailed/fresh/ready or Jezebel, girls across racial lines know and understand what it means to be considered sexually promiscuous and treated as a social pariah as if (perceived) sexual desires will infect others. However, because of the intersections of race, youth, socioeconomic status, body development, perceived attitude, and geographic positioning, the experiences that Black girls have serve as the basis for considerations of Black women's hypersexuality.

Not only do the sexual scripts that Cooper, Durham, and Douglas identify in (southern) Black cultural spaces maintain the construction of Black women and girls as Jezebels, freaks, and video hos, but they even translate beyond spaces where Black girls are explicitly sexual. When a Black girl is present, the mere semblance of romantic chemistry is deemed sexual because her body is always already imbued with ideas of sexual depravity via the sexual scripts that circulate through cultural productions and institutions. This so-called sign of Black girls' sexual degeneration echoes scholar Darieck Scott's explanation of how the West configures blackness as abjection or "a repository for fears about sexuality and death—fears, in other words, about the difficulty of maintaining the boundaries of the (white male) ego ... an invention that accomplishes the domination of those who bear it as an identity."[22] Blackness and femaleness thus confer sexual promiscuity onto Black girls by just existing. The foundation for (southern Black Christian) Mother's Day sermons as well as attitudes toward Black girls is this simple axiom: a Black female—regardless of age—is sexually unhinged and in need of discipline.

Keke, Do You Love Me? Romance for Black Girls

Alongside these larger cultural discourses, then, the development of Micah and Keke's relationship in season 1 of *Queen Sugar*, as written and directed by Black women, is remarkable. While the adults in the show seem to be haunted by death, historical and contemporary barriers to success, and systems like incarceration that maintain stark contrasts for Black, Latinx, Asian, Native, and white people in the South, Micah and Keke's love seems to blossom uninterrupted and with little drama outside of Micah's relocation to Saint Josephine Parish from Los Angeles. And yet, DuVernay's casting and construction of this budding love is particularly interesting for reasons such as its divergence from the eponymous book from which the show is derived, cultivation of self-assuredness in Keke's character in season 1, and the navigation of cultural specificities between Micah and Keke that further illustrate the discourses through which DuVernay wades throughout the season.

The author of the book on which the show *Queen Sugar* is based, Natalie Baszile, characterizes Micah as an eleven-year-old girl and presents the overall complexity of the narrative as one based in a mother-daughter story of love and self-determination. These two distinctions (although there are many others) between the book and the television series allow the viewers to participate in a narrative rarely presented on television or film: the beginnings of romantic love between two Black teens that is respectful, loving, and nonviolent. DuVernay's editorial shift to allow viewers to see the blossoming of a romantic relationship between Micah and Keke exhibits the creative involvement of DuVernay. More broadly, it exhibits the ways that Black women in creative leadership roles like hers imagine and participate in the discourse of Black romantic love for Black girls who are culturally deemed unlovable because of their licentious and depraved ways. The conferral of sexual promiscuity onto

Black girls generally means respectful and reciprocal love is not possible for them because they are undeserving. DuVernay and her team consider the development of love for Black girls in the face of perceived promiscuity based on race, gender, and youth as well as a world constructed through racism and various violent encounters. In a world where representations of southern Black girls (particularly those who are treated with love and respect) are still rare to behold, *Queen Sugar* presents remarkable possibilities for the ways that Black girls are seen.

Despite the palpable beauty of their interactions in the scene I described in episode 9, social media commentators characterized Keke as a flirty "fast girl" who aggressively pursues Micah and "moves too fast" for her "shy" beau. Some users' characterizations of Keke turned misogynoir as they quickly used "fast" to demarcate Keke's self-assuredness as abnormal for girls (or boys) of her age. For example, on November 9, 2016, @_foreverkenny says pointedly that "this girl [Keke] on queen sugar fast." Another user, @manifestfaith, takes it a step further when they tweet, "Normally you would find a city boy fast and fresh and a country girl shy but on queen sugar it's versa vice. #queensugar."

These comments, all made by users with Black women avatar profile pictures, rest not only on the idea that Keke's direct questions and answers with Micah are illustrative of some sexual depravity but also on the idea that she is somehow going against the norms and attitudes that girls, especially Black girls, should exhibit when meeting a "city boy." Her self-assuredness and unwillingness to allow misinterpretation or confusion to be the basis of their budding romance is characterized as "fast," "fresh," and "sass"—words specifically lauded at Black girls who speak up. Corrosively, these social media characterizations illustrate the ways in which contemporary discussions of sexuality—while they have advanced in some ways beyond compulsory heterosexuality and men's pleasure—continue to construct Black girls as always already hypersexual and overassertive.

These cultural attitudes frame Keke and other Black girls who determine their interactions with others as "fast-tailed girls," constructing Black girls' coming-of-age experiences with love and sexuality as lewd and lascivious. While Keke joked and asked questions, her interactions with Micah were little more than teenage bravado for a southern Black girl. Micah's inability to play the dozens too or ask any questions about Keke's background creates a juxtaposition between the ways that Keke's and Micah's engagement is read. When contrasted with Micah's shyness and no clear initiation in conversation from him in these scenes, commentators reframed Keke's comments as something other than innocent.

The regional and cultural differences in their upbringing, however, underlie their interactions. Keke's jokes and comments are situated in a southern Black context in which people speak directly (with a smile, of course) regardless of how curt it may seem. Episode 10 opens with Micah sitting in the bleachers, watching Keke's drill team practice.[23] For him to show up at her school's early morning activities illustrates the same initiative and attitude that Keke has in the last episode, yet it goes unremarked upon in social media responses to the show. Keke jokes, again, that Micah should enroll in school "cuz I see your SAT scores droppin by the day" and after some conversation about schools shyly asks him to confirm his interest in her: "Let me know how that goes . . . if you not clappin for somebody else."[24] This is the first time that Micah's steady gaze goes elsewhere briefly. When it returns he says, "I'm gonna let you go. Guess I'll see you soon" with an inquisitive tone and a slight arch of his right brow. Keke says, "Why guess when you can know? Micah, you are long overdue for some company." He nods in agreement and again drops his gaze. Keke offers, "I'll drop by Ms. Violet's house after school. This ain't gon be no Netflix and Chill kinda situation." Micah knowingly laughs at the reference and says, "No no, of course not."[25] They stare at each other a while, then Keke clears her throat eyeing the door—indicating to Micah that he should open the door for her. He swiftly obliges and looks at her as she walks away.

While Keke is quick to make jokes with Micah, he (in a southern Black context) would be considered technically the aggressor in this scene. Since their first interaction was a spontaneous meeting at which Micah questions whether he will see Keke again, Micah communicates his interest in Keke and his intent to create situations where they interact (rather than allowing them to be spontaneous as she derides by saying "Why guess when you could know") by showing up to her practice and waiting to speak to her afterwards. Keke's invitation to drop by Vi's house is a positive affirmation of Micah's forwardness, communicating to both of them that she is interested in getting to know him more, even as she jokes about his SAT scores. Keke's invitation pointedly communicates what her presence consents (or rather does not consent) to, but more importantly, that she appreciates and plans to reciprocate Micah's forwardness. While neither Micah nor Keke are new to dating, they both illustrate a planned and concerted effort to communicate their interest in respectable ways, such as planning to see each other in public spaces and where adults or other teenagers will be present. Keke's mention of "Netflix and Chill" further cements the respectable interactions she expects and how she demarcates "good" and "fast" girl behavior. A euphemism for sexual intercourse or at least intimate sexual acts while watching television, "Netflix and Chill" and Keke's refusal of that "kinda situation" communicates the seriousness with which she hopes Micah's interest in her is blossoming. Even as audiences might misread her joking nature or body language as forwardness, the regional specificities of their relationship further instantiate the respectability that DuVernay crafts in the ways Keke interacts with Micah as well as, more generally, how Black girls' self-assuredness through jokes and slick phrases belie teenage angst or awkwardness. Additionally, the cultural space between Micah's wealthy Los Angeles lifestyle (and the predominately white preparatory school he attended) and Keke's southern Black upbringing encourages a more distinct interpretation of their interactions that does not rely on misogynoir.

The regional specificities of their relationship play out further in episode 12, when Micah and Keke officially become a couple after kissing a few times and walking to and from Keke's school together.

Keke makes it clear that "kissing [her] all the damn time" is only justified in the context of a relationship, to which Micah replies "Alright."[26] Now that they are a "thing," she reminds him that he needs to come over to her house for dinner and meet her father, Boogie. Micah's confusion of why he must meet her father again is cleared up when she says, "Have you ever dated a Black girl before? You in the Souf now. . . . When you date a Black girl, you meet her daddy. He makes sure you got manners and put a lil fear in ya."[27] This conversation illustrates that social mores of the South, especially for Black girls, are dictated by patriarchal influence codified as protection—part of the ideological work Lomax explains undergirds the Black Church's commitment to Black patriarchs and the nuclear family; a father's job in this situation is to drive off any boys who do not have good intentions by exerting his masculinity (usually showing off weapons or bodily strength) against the interested boy. The meeting of father and boyfriend, then, represents an age-old exchange of power between men, even while women create and facilitate this exchange. A Black girl, in particular, who wants to exude respectability and encourage her new beau to present himself to her with love and care *must* have a patriarchal figure for whom boys will express their initial interest (and later, marital intentions).

In this way, Black women and Black girls maintain patriarchal power dynamics in southern Black contexts. Reflecting on her own upbringing, Brittney Cooper reminds us that "Black women pay the highest costs for investing in respectability politics," of which I understand the meeting of father and beau as an important structural component to the maintenance of respectability.[28] She further remarks, "We (middle-class women) are taught those women, who were once 'fast-tailed girls' make us all look bad. . . . I knew early on that I didn't want to be like the girls in my middle school, saddled with children I couldn't support and doomed to a lifetime of low-wage work with little opportunity for advancement."[29] The correlation between "fast" girls and low-wage work or multiple pregnancies in her statement illustrates the very social, economic, and geopolitical structure, both discursive and cultural, that we create for Black girls when we use "fast" to describe self-determination and confidence. Outside the purview of a patriarch, which Imani Perry explains is inextricably tied to ownership and the control of people as property, Black girls' self-determination is only intelligible as fast.[30] Black girls, too, are taught to circumscribe their own agency and desires by channeling all their decisions through their fathers or other patriarchs.

Therefore, Keke's instruction of and insistence on Micah's visit to her family's dinner table to meet her father sketches the contours of Black girls' adherence to the politics of respectability. Beyond the Christian presuppositions that encourage Black girls to participate in the maintenance of patriarchal power in their lives, Keke's insistence traces the ways that Black girls learn that they may be protected from social scorn, economic scarcity, and (supposedly) gendered violence. With permission from her father, Keke is allowed to "properly" date Micah and protect herself from the very words and phrases that social media users lauded at her early on. Emblematic of interracial and intraracial anxieties about Black girls' sexual depravity built on racist and sexist ideas, Keke's adherence to social mores about dating recognize how adult Black women and men especially would view her as a dark-skinned Black girl teenager.

Although season 1 ends with greater insight into the pitfalls and possibilities available to the Bordelon family for the harvest of their sugarcane, Micah and Keke's relationship and the larger framework from which to understand their interactions as well as the social media responses to them typify the sexual scripts, the cultural discourses, and the regional specificities that govern Black girls' social and cultural outlook in real life. Keke's disparagement makes evident the pressures that impede Black girls' self-actualization.

Fast Black Girls IRL?

While Keke is a fictional character constructed through the eyes of Black women directors and writers who wanted to illustrate the possibilities of trust, love, and affection for dark-skinned Black girls on screen, the discursive framing of Black girls as fast is present in many aspects of Black girls' adolescence. Considered cunning and artful in the ways that they supposedly rush into sexual interactions with boys and men, Black girls face harsh criticism for the ways they dress, speak, or behave whether at home or in public spaces. Especially for southern Black girls, the threat of being called fast looms large in school classrooms or social environments, in the comfort of their bedrooms, and in church or other religious settings.

The positioning of Black girls socially and culturally as fast is undergirded by patriarchal attitudes that let men, especially Black men, traumatize them with little repercussions. In the infamous case of singer-producer Robert Kelly ("R. Kelly"), for example, Black girls who reported the sexual assault they suffered at his hands were dismissed, demonized, and mistreated for over three decades.[31] Even as dream hampton's documentary *Surviving R. Kelly* (2019) detailed the ordeals of girls as young as twelve, men and women used words like "fast" to describe the girls in both Chicago and Atlanta who spoke out about their experiences with Kelly.[32] Chicago—as one of the main locations for Black southerners to move during the Great Migration and a continued geographic space of Black excellence and pride—not only has a social connectedness to Atlanta, but through Kelly's abuse, illustrates the widespread implications of Black southern constructions of Black girls as fast.

While Chicago was once the place where southern Black girls were sent to secure protection from the wandering eyes and hands of white vigilantes in the early twentieth century—or, as sociologist Tressie McMillan Cottom explains, a place to which Black women and girls "were escaping black men who drank too much and sometimes touched little girls too long in ways that were both wrong and acceptable"—this same location becomes the site of Kelly's predation and entrapment of Black girls.[33] Therefore, the geographical space between Georgia and Illinois belies the Black geospatial legacies that supposedly brought protection and prosperity to Black girls and their families. This traveling signification of Black girls as hypersexual extends across physical and digital space, time, and politics;

said differently, Black girls are scolded for their perceived sexual indiscretions regardless of the location, their age, the time period, or the individuals involved. Through the ways that Kelly's victims were discounted and ridiculed by celebrities and those within the Black community—while many of the same people supported white women victims who came forward against Hollywood producer Harvey Weinstein—other Black girls witnessed as their community hurled rape culture axioms (such as "what was she wearing?") and fast girl ideologies to justify why Kelly's music, career, and life should still be supported.[34] While Jim DeRogatis, who released the first story about Kelly in December 2000, notes his knowledge of forty-eight Black girls who experienced sexual abuse and violence from Kelly, Sheila Baldwin argues these girls "have bought into the misogynistic behavior that Black men have exhibited toward them. They've adopted the label of whore and ho. They've adopted the label of bitch—that's what they call themselves. They get beat up and they think that's love. Finally, they are sexually abused and they accept that that is just a relationship."[35] While I bristle at the idea that Black girls between the ages of eleven and eighteen knowingly accept and call themselves misogynistic names, I know that fast Black girl ideologies entangle them in the same systems where they are taught that men like Kelly solely create the conditions within which their bodies can be acceptably sexual.

Black girls learn that their bodies are not their own; and, when Black girls try to dictate for themselves what their bodies look like or how their bodies behave, the socially descriptive force of fast is not far behind, regardless of the men who stare longingly at their budding breasts, hips, and buttocks. Teetering constantly on the verge of being called fast, and knowing the ramifications for being considered fast by anyone, Black girls like those Kelly scouted while at school or getting food as well as Black girls like me who are approached by men twice their age while at the mall or at work know that the world does not care about what happens to them nor what these men do to them. Even girls who are groomed by older boys and men through lavish gifts or sexual comments about their bodies are encouraged to accept these favors as evidence of worthiness, yet they are called fast when pregnancies occur from their rapes. Fast becomes the explanation for the webs Black men create to entangle their next underage sexual conquest and for all the hurt, pain, and confusion that saddle so-called fast Black girls (and their supposedly not fast friends) on their way to womanhood. Fast becomes the culprit in statistics about teenage pregnancies, unwed mothers, and the Moynihan-esque arguments about the destruction of the Black family. Fastness and the Black girls who feel the brunt of its force thus supposedly stand in the way of Black progress and community cohesiveness.[36] In short, it is said and felt that fast Black girls (hos/Jezebels/whores/sluts) ruin us all.

A Rose Is Still a Rose: Loving Black Girls

The digital conversation surrounding Keke, especially as a dark-complexioned teenage girl in the southern US, represents a cultural attitude of misogynoir that impedes Black girls' ability to be confident, self-possessed, and direct about what it means to know them and love them fully. The cultural discourses and sexual scripts based in Black religious and cultural understanding of Black women and girls harm Black girls by framing the ways they express confidence in their appearance, proximity to puberty, and ability to articulate their interests and desires as "fast" rather than as self-determination or self-love. Whether fictional or not, and across geospatial or temporal boundaries, Black girls are consistently confronted by ideas that chastise them for being themselves.

Cultural concerns about Black girls' morality and purity date back to the turn of the twentieth century when Black intellectuals, sorority women, and uplift organizers cited the dangers of Black girls' sexual depravity as the greatest danger to the future of their lives as "New Negroes."[37] Black women, especially, were involved in crafting organizations and institutions that would help direct "wayward" girls and position them to better the race.[38] Unfortunately, our narratives around Black girlhood and directed to Black girls about their bodies have not shifted. The cultural attitudes that frame Black girls' hair, clothes, bodies, and verbal expression as fast are imbedded in longer histories of Black respectability and uplift politics that use Black girls as the moral compass of the race because of their potential to become "race mothers."[39] Like the social media commentators who remarked upon Keke, we continue to proliferate ideas of Black girls as "freaks" and "hos" because of patriarchal sexual scripts based in misogynoir and so-called religious doctrine.[40] Historian Tanisha Ford explains,

> Being fast wasn't just about sex. It had little to do with sex, because not all girls who were openly having sex were made to wear the scarlet F. Being fast had as much to do with the fact that some adults fear that your curiosity about "grown folks' dealings" was too dangerous for your own good, a curiosity that would render the adults powerless to protect you from the world. Some also feared that you would outpace them in life, learn more, experience more. And if you did that, how could they ever communicate with you, relate to you, manage you, control you? So they hurled out words like fast, which stung when they hit, more so out of their own fear and insecurities than as a way to name our "bad" behavior. Some of our folks would rather throw us girls away than grapple with their own brokenness.[41]

As Ford points out, the purpose for hurling words like fast at Black girls is based in adult desires to control Black girls rather than understand them. Importantly, too, the use of fast disguises adults' trauma from their own adolescent mistreatment and sexual abuse as well as their continued inability (or unwillingness) to challenge men like R. Kelly who continue to harm, abuse, and violate Black girls and women, along with the sanctity of community or family. As Black women who live with, raise, teach, and exist in community with Black girls, we must reconsider what it means to craft identities for those Black girls that mirror the way US society constructs us every day. We must find ways to re-engineer how we are always perceived as too-something in the ways that our coworkers, lovers, and strangers construct our armor of blackness and womanness. By loving our own fast-tailed girl selves, we allow and facilitate Black girls' vision of their current and future selves as full human beings.

By identifying the ways we fail in our personal interactions with Black girls, we can better locate the failures that occur in popular films. How we characterize Black girls through social and theological explanations spills over into the entertainment we enjoy at home, and it is not a coincidence that Black girls are abused and violated on screen, too. In the films I discuss throughout the rest of the book, we see failure erupting in almost every interaction with Black girls. They are more visible through hypervisibility as the central characters in these stories, and yet the harm they experience is justified as necessary plot structures. These films show that Black girls' experiences of violence and abuse from surveillance, perceived sexuality and haughtiness, and patriarchal influence are required for the narrative to unfold and for other characters to evolve. Such films have further circulated our failures and made us all more complicit in Black girls' mistreatment. And yet, Black girls continue to show how accountability to oneself first has the potential to shape everything and everyone around them, even alongside our continued failures of priority, commitment, and recognition on the silver screen.

CHAPTER 4

Black Girls Save the World

> At fifteen years old, I should be focusing on school, cheerleading, and just being a normal kid. Instead, I've spent over half my life fighting for the most basic human right: access to clean, safe drinking water.
>
> —Amariyanna "Little Miss Flint" Copeny

In the past decade, girl saviors have become a reoccurring depiction. While real life girl saviors exist through global media surveillance as activists who argue for social, economic, and ecological justice, Black girls' participation in political agitation is rarely assessed in this way. The girl activist as savior garners support through perceived innocence and harmlessness; girls like Greta Thunberg and Ahed Tamimi are recognized for their work to end injustice to the environment and are believed to be doing *more* than what is required of a young, innocent child.[1] However, girls like Amariyanna "Little Miss Flint" Copeny go unremarked upon despite her fighting for infrastructure reform and clean water for Flint, Michigan residents for more than a decade. Even when then-President Barack Obama visited Flint in 2016 to learn about the situation after eight-year-old Copeny wrote a letter, he jokingly drank a glass of tap water and asked if anyone was thirsty, further ostracizing Copeny and the Flint communities she has been advocating for since elementary school. Since then, Copeny posts monthly about the elapsed time since Flint has been without adequate drinking water and has raised thousands of dollars for clean water, books for children in her community, and she has advocated for help from private water companies to assist Flint.

Copeny, however, is rarely regarded as working for environmental justice or part of the activism girls globally have undertaken around the contemporary climate crisis. Despite her visibility due to social media and her letter that prompted Obama's 2016 visit, Copeny's struggle to attain clean water for her family and friends is a failure in two parts: First, her childhood has been marked by the failure of US infrastructure to help and protect its citizens, ultimately leading to a dystopian geological landscape for Black people. Second, her experience illustrates a failure of recognition and prioritization by a community, so much so that a young Black girl feels compelled to intervene. Black girls like Copeny have been advocating for everything from environmental justice and protections on reproductive rights to safety from gun violence and sexual abuse visibly in the media for decades, yet their counterparts are recognized as true girl activists. Black girls "carr[y] the weight of economic anxieties and political uncertainties" and are considered "either surplus or productive in the context of social service."[2] Copeny's advocacy and activism is then considered a typical part of Black girlhood and therefore unremarkable or "surplus" in shifting a world away from social, economic, and environmental collapse.

Stereotypes of Black girls in popular culture have received less analytical attention yet feature similar characteristics to that of Copeny. Because others consider their work against dystopia to be common for Black girls (a failure of recognition and a symptom of racism), the stereotypes create the cultural dynamic that Black girls are superheroes and saviors of others even against their own self-interest. As Copeny's quote remarks in the opening epigraph to this chapter, Black girls "should be focusing on school . . . and just being a normal kid" yet they spend their lives "fighting for the most basic human right." This is a catastrophic failure that has been regurgitated in several critically acclaimed films. Two examples that I find particularly egregious in their presentation of Black girls as salvific despite the abuse and harm they receive are Melanie in *The Girl with All the Gifts* and Hushpuppy in *Beasts of the Southern Wild*.

Melanie and Hushpuppy are both set in worlds of lack, places that their caretakers are regularly absent from or unhelpful in. As Black girls at the end of the world, in complexly different ways, Melanie and Hushpuppy present young Black girl figures as brave, curious, deeply connected to others, and consistently protective of the adults in their lives. They are Black girl saviors in how they are constantly working to keep other people alive, to take care of the places they consider home, and to map a vision of the world in their own image. While the adults around them are unreliable and refuse the full responsibilities of care that these girls require, Melanie and Hushpuppy show others in their communities the way to freedom.

The films themselves use Black girls to create empathy for the adults (many times, white) who are struggling within these contexts. Repeatedly, Black girls are presented as the balm to the rude, despondent, and dystopic adults in their midst. They are representative of and characterize hope, even as the dialogue, scenes, and film narrative present the adults as proxy for the audience. We are supposed to side with the adults and similarly use the Black girls as receptacles for our anxieties, even as they are the sources of our entertainment.

In what follows, I contextualize the representations of Black girl saviors, like Melanie and Hushpuppy, within a larger framework of misogynoir that always presents Black girls as salvific yet mean and disposable. Despite Hollywood's obsession with using Black girl characters to communicate white animosities, anxieties, and stereotypes, Black girls continue to revamp what Black girlhood looks like on screen. Melanie and Hushpuppy push us to consider how Black girls animate different ways of being through their rejection of white attitudes and adults' desires.

Dystopia's Savior: Melanie and the Hungries

In a world where dystopia seems more fact than fiction and in a genre that depicts zombies as emotionless and mindless, a film like *The Girl with All the Gifts* (2016) differs greatly. Written by Mike Carey (M. R. Carey) based on his well-received book of the same name,

The Girl with All the Gifts presents a world overtaken by a fungal virus. Spread through saliva (and I assume other human secretions), the fungus inhabits the brains of its symbiotic carrier. Described as wrapping itself around its host's brain like an ivy on a tree, the fungus rapidly requires feeding, enhancing the animalistic desire to hunt and feed until satiated. Those who succumb to the fungus become idle, swaying in groups together like tall grass in a breeze. Once activated by the smell of food, loud noise, or swift movement, the people who have succumbed to the virus turn into "hungries." They subsequently eat others who turn into hungries as well, spreading the fungus to more and more hosts.

Based outside London twenty years after the virus has taken over, the film starts at a military base. While the narrative arc of the book relies on the empathy and intimacy created between Melanie—a young white girl—and her teacher, Miss Justineau (her "very dark skin" teacher), the film reverses this relationship. Melanie (Sennia Nanua) and her teacher, Miss Justineau (Gemma Arterton), form a kindred bond that propels the arc of the film and in many ways humanizes the hungries. Specifically, through the ways that Justineau empathizes and cares deeply for Melanie, the other hungries—particularly those who are not directly threatening the lives of their group—are seen as smart, engaging, and suffering people. Featuring a young Black girl, though, the film's course shifts from the book's desire to humanize zombies in a postapocalyptic landscape.

As the only Black child, let alone Black female, shown throughout the film, Melanie's character serves to reinforce ideas about blackness as superhuman and fantastical as well as simple, animalistic, and primitive simultaneously. The scenes showing her cunningly distract hungries or protect Justineau while under threat are juxtaposed with the painstakingly slow, gory images of her eating people or animals to satisfy hunger. Since there's little evidence of other hungries' reaction after eating, Melanie's lethargic response to satisfying her hunger throughout the film is shot in a way that creates a type of malaise, which can be read as laziness (known as "the itis" in Black vernacular). Taken together, Melanie's animalistic protectiveness and highly creative and inquisitive personality mark her as not only different than hungries (or even hybrid children like her) but also different than all the people she interacts with, especially Justineau. While Melanie in many ways is presented as the victor at the end of the film, Justineau's ethic of care for children generally and for Melanie, in particular, is the noteworthy takeaway. Because of Justineau's care and concern, she is spared when all others become hungries after Melanie burns the skyscraper-sized viral pod tree in the middle of the city. The underlying ideology, much like those of white savior films popularized in the 1990s and early 2000s, is that ultimately white people are inherently good; they will be cared for and protected, even when they do despicable things; and at the end of the world, they will still be the victors. Even after the world ends and everyone is a zombie, white women like Justineau always survive.

Hollywood's Colorblind Casting: An Imaginative Force of White Supremacy

The reverse casting of Justineau and Melanie—who were Black and white in the book, yet white and Black in the film—produces a completely different racialized progression of the story arc. The dynamic created in the book, where the audience is introduced to a Black woman teacher who is showing care and attention to a white girl zombie, forces us to consider new ways of seeing both Black women (who are historically characterized as unfeeling and uneducated) and white girls (who since *Uncle Tom's Cabin* have been the personification of innocence). Historian Robin Bernstein argues that all children learn early who has the privilege of being innocent, while education scholar Monique Morris and anthropologist Savannah Shange note the adultification of Black girls results in lifelong challenges including carceral punishment, even in politically progressive environments.[3] Therefore, the characterization of Black girl as zombie and white woman as (white female) savior activates longstanding tropes in Hollywood and global popular culture.

The author/screenwriter of *The Girl with All the Gifts*, Mike Carey, explains that the main character, Melanie, "is a young girl who has grown up in extraordinary conditions. She lives in a subterranean bunker on an army base. Her experience of the world is limited to a handful of rooms and a corridor. She doesn't question this. It's all she's ever known. But we notice she's being treated in a very strange way by the adults around her, that she's treated like a cross between a wild beast and an unexploded bomb."[4] The producer Cammie Gatin goes on to say that the film uses the beliefs about childhood innocence to trick the audience; she says, "It's all about tricking the audience into feeling a lot of empathy for these children and then revealing that these children are, in fact, monsters. And they don't even know it themselves."[5] In auditioning actresses, Gatin explains she was looking for a little girl who had the "stamina" to work in a "derelict environment" for ten weeks with adult actors when she's in every scene. It is obvious they had not planned to cast a Black girl. They were looking for a child that could withstand long days, take direction, and help the audience feel the empathic impulse of the film and book, which forces people to consider a child monster (a zombie that could eat people with little concern) as more than just a monster. The "trick" of empathy is even more salient when they hire Sennia Nanua to play Melanie.

Situating Black Girlhood: Does It Matter That Melanie Is Black?

Some might argue that the shift from white girl to Black girl is of little consequence to the film. However, the first page of Carey's novel makes the change that much more problematic:

> Her name is Melanie. It means "the black girl," from an ancient Greek word, but her skin is actually very fair so she thinks maybe it's not such a good name for her. She likes the name Pandora a whole lot, but you don't get to choose.... Now she's ten years old, and she has skin like a princess in a fairy

tale; skin as white as snow. So she knows that when she grows up she'll be beautiful, with princes falling over themselves to climb her tower and rescue her.[6]

Later, when Miss Justineau is introduced in the book, Carey's pointed racialized language resurfaces. With Melanie as our narrator, we learn,

> Miss Justineau's face stands out anyway because it's such a wonderful, wonderful colour. It's dark brown, like the wood of the trees in Melanie's rainforest picture whose seeds only grow out of the ashes of a bushfire, or like the coffee that Miss Justineau pours out of her flask into her cup at break time. Except it's darker and richer than either of those things, with lots of other colours mixed in, so there isn't anything you can really compare it to. All you can say is that it's as dark as Melanie's skin is light.[7]

There are few other descriptions of others' skin in the first chapter of the book. While Miss Justineau's skin is supposedly incomparable, Carey finds comparison with wood and coffee first. He then reminds the reader, in Melanie's own voice although she speaks in third person, that Miss Justineau is on the complete opposite side of the color spectrum from Melanie. While there may be no description to match Miss Justineau's "darker, richer" skin, we know that Melanie is "white as snow," "like a princess in a fairy tale," and will eventually be beautiful for no other fact than she is white. As much as we are made to understand Melanie's affinity for Miss Justineau's "wonderful colour," Carey makes it clear that she is not a princess, she is not beautiful, she is as dark as Melanie is light. While Melanie's name is "the black girl," it does not fit her very white, very snowy, very princess-like color. Therefore, her name, one apparently assigned by Miss Justineau, does not fit. She would rather her name be "Pandora," from the Greek mythological origin story Miss Justineau read to them that describes the first woman on earth who opens a box and "lets terrible things out." Given gifts from the gods like charm, beauty, and cleverness, Pandora's name is supposedly better suited for our "white as snow" protagonist/narrator.

The casting of Sennia Nanua then is not accidental or without meaning. Putting a (fair skinned) Black girl child into the role of zombie savior not only elides the problematic racial politics of the book, but it also further imbues the character with historical discourses of blackness, racism, and childhood. For example, as early as the fifteenth century Black girls were used as counterpoints to white girls' beauty, daintiness, and civilized nature; Black girls were considered vectors of disease, ugly, beastly, and representative of excess.[8] In a fantastical world where the line between societal ruin and civilization is the military base on which we meet Melanie—seemingly the only Black girl child left in the world and the only child still able to separate her hunger for flesh from her love for all things creative, beautiful, and mythological—the audience is supposed to be surprised and horrified by Melanie's treatment because she is a child. However, the historical representation of Black girls as monstrous and excessive makes her treatment normal and therefore necessary for the safety of the white people she is around as well as to the progression of the narrative. By simply being friendly, caring, and curious, Melanie is both childlike and beyond her years. Her petite frame and fair complexion are supposed to mark her as non-threatening, until of course her appetite needs to be satiated. Then the horror of her monstrous nature makes her treatment justifiable.

This characterization of Black children generally, and Black girls in particular, is not new. Both in literature and historical discourses, there are countless examples of Black girls being used as counterpoints to the civility, beauty, and angelic personalities of white children. Historian of early American childhood Crystal Webster explains that in the nineteenth century, childhood itself was used to mark Black people as incapable of caring for themselves and as justification for indentured servitude until they turned twenty-eight, even after the end of slavery.[9] Similarly, historians of Black childhood LaKisha Simmons and Kabria Baumgartner show that because Black girls were constantly represented as licentious, wild, and unkempt in the twentieth century, they were illustrative of the need for greater restrictions of Black freedom and access to education both in northern states and across the South.[10] Literary scholar Habiba Ibrahim argues that age itself was always constructed outside of and beyond blackness; she explains that "when the (white) viewer sees 'blackness' projected onto the other, what is *not seen* is normative, human age. What the white viewer sees is black children with adorable faces and fully grown bodies . . . or the white viewer sees a monstrosity that could be of any age."[11] This monstrous imagining of Black children, and in this case a Black girl, maintains centuries' old narratives about Black people and their inability to be fully formed and therefore supported and protected citizenry. From the origins of John Locke's personhood in the seventeenth century, Black people have been excluded or in excess of what (or rather who) is considered right, just, worthy, and protected.[12] Whether in educational settings or in dystopian environments of decay and fear, Black children are too loud, too curious, too much for the world around them. Without age due to their skin being melanated, Black children like Melanie represent the fullness of white fear—a monster that has no order or purpose other than to feed on their families, their lives, and their dreams.

The fear of Black children has led to the murder of many Black girls and boys. In fictive, dystopian spaces like *The Girl with All the Gifts*, Hollywood has created a savior to protect the world from them. The savior is always noble, always caring, always smart—always white.

Hollywood's White Savior Problem

The pairing of white woman teacher and Black child in need of saving is a Hollywood trope long perfected. Like previous white savior films that as a genre depict white people helping those less fortunate by aligning themselves (via politics, money, or families) with those in need, this film doubles down. This idea is even more salient in apocalyptic settings where everyone is supposedly only concerned about themselves and their family's survival. While the film encourages empathy for the Black "monster" using Nanua's petite frame and fair complexion as well as her character's intelligence and kindness for others within an apocalyptic setting, it eventually pushes the audience to translate empathy from monster to the white savior at the end of the film.

Film scholar Justin Gomer argues that Hollywood is specifically invested in the white savior genre to center whiteness even as sociopolitical discourses dictate an allegiance to colorblind ideology. According to Gomer, "teacher films," which arose in the late 1990s and early 2000s, "rely heavily on old tropes of Hollywood melodrama... as well as racialized discourses about black and Latinx families from the post-Moynihan and Reagan years... offer[ing] the neoliberal colorblind solution to the problems of urban America."[13] Reimagining the past and renegotiating racialized discourses in the present, Gomer's "teacher films" illustrate the need for white people in Black and Latinx environments to stave off the pathological cycles of savagery. White women teachers, through their moral crusade to "save" the savage, undisciplined, and uneducated children in their classrooms, are presented as "victim-heroes"—victims because their white counterparts and families do not approve of their commitment to their students, and heroes because their presence alone illustrates that these students need disciplined, dedicated teachers (the domestic version of civilizing missionaries) rather than governmental intervention.[14]

While the book does not follow this trope, the casting choices in *The Girl with All the Gifts* regurgitate the prerogatives of the "teacher film" even in a dystopic environment. Whereas the backdrop of the film shows a world ravaged by a virus and its hosts, the teacher-student dynamic that opens the film is maintained throughout. Melanie is constantly asking questions of those around her and pushing them to reconsider their militaristic and inhumane response to her and her classmates (who are all white boys). Melanie's particular affinity for Miss Justineau further substantiates her importance as Melanie's savior—Justineau repeatedly protects and humanizes Melanie while her colleagues use fear and coercive force to study and control her. Again, this positioning is specific to this Hollywood adaptation, proving that whether past, present, or future, whiteness and white women, specifically, are *our* moral compass and therefore should be protected at all costs.

Neoliberal colorblind ideology would encourage us to see Justineau and Melanie as two individuals brought together by mere circumstance to care deeply about one another. However, the racial politics of the film—evidenced by the extreme whiteness of the cast, apart from Melanie and two Black men soldiers, who both die after being eaten by hungries—shifts the racial focus of the book and forces us to consider two concepts in film theory that impact our understanding of this film but also the racial dynamics in film culture largely. Film and media scholar Kristen Warner's "plastic representation" and education researcher Ebony Elizabeth Thomas's "the dark fantastic" argue that the racial politics inherent in casting Black people in roles originally written and cast for white people are more concerning than liberatory. Whereas marginalized people have argued for greater representation in visual culture since the rise of vaudeville and blackface minstrelsy, the casting of Black people in so-called race-neutral roles begs greater attention.

While many consider greater skin color and body diversity in film as a marker of progress in racial politics, Warner argues that the simple construction of positive and negative representation allows Hollywood executives to ignore developing robust and complex characters of color by simply hiring a few actors of colors in race-neutral roles. She calls this phenomenon "plastic representation" because it "uses the wonder that comes from seeing characters on screen who serve as visual identifiers for specific demographics to flatten the expectation to desire anything more."[15] In many ways, these visual identifiers are not built into characters' development, but rather are simply a sign of an actor being hired to play a particular role. The character is made representational because of the actor who is playing them, blurring the distinction between character and actor, allowing the mimesis of film to occur supposedly by accident. The actor's blackness becomes a marker of visual diversity; therefore, any cultural recognition that may occur for the audience is based on the actor's phenotype and cultural background rather than the character's. This distinction matters and is palpable as the character "is not adjusted for the person of color who is hired [and] they become vulnerable to unintended stereotypes and tropes attached to the cultural and historical experiences tethered to their bodies."[16] This plays out somewhat differently for Melanie and Justineau because of how Carey writes each character in highly racialized ways—"white as snow" and "as black as [Melanie is] white"—despite their difference in the film. For example, depicting a white girl as a half-person, half-zombie, as highly educated and curious while also animalistic and always on the verge of cannibalistic desire, as Carey does in the book, has a different racial resonance than the same depiction in the body of a Black girl. Especially because the narration of the book transfers seamlessly between Melanie and an omnipresent narrator, the beliefs, motivations, and desires of Melanie are made more apparent than in the film that presents Melanie as a lead character, but not the voice through which we understand the narrative. Because of the histories of Black people, especially enslaved Africans, depicted as zombies or "zombified" for the purposes of racialized political and economic commentary, the casting of Melanie as a Black girl who opens the box of horrors to the world like Pandora is not race-neutral.[17]

We watch Melanie follow a particular cycle as we are introduced to her throughout the film—first as a highly intelligent, curious, and courteous young Black girl who is for some reason in a prison and held back with restraints. This cycle maps onto what Thomas's "dark fantastic" attempts to explain as the "the role that racial difference plays in our fantastically storied imaginations."[18] The cycle of engagement with dark-skinned people in fantastical narratives includes five stages: "(1) spectacle, (2) hesitation, (3) violence, (4) haunting, and (5) emancipation"; this cycle purportedly allows the myth of these narratives to "feel true" because the racial logics undergirding social relations in the present are upheld even in fantasy and fairy tales, even though they are more complicated in our present lived experiences.[19] As we watch Melanie, we see hesitation, violence, and haunting occur as the film progresses: hesitation when Melanie almost bites Miss Justineau; violence when she is held captive with a mask and restraints while others run and flee; haunting when she is finally freed to feed; then emancipation when she sets fire to the virus's host plant in the middle of town—freeing herself from the mask and restraints, and in turn reversing the freedom Miss Justineau experiences for that of her own. As the audience, though, we are supposed to side with the forlorn Miss Justineau who cries one single tear when she realizes there is no future for her outside of her containment facility.

Even though her character is a white girl in the novel, Melanie's character in *The Girl with All the Gifts* film illustrates Thomas's cycle of engagement precisely because of Hollywood's own dedication to create, regurgitate, and mythically recast neoliberal colorblind narratives as natural and normal, as commonsense. As Stuart Hall explains, commonsense "helps us to classify the world in simple but meaningful terms.... Common sense does not require reasoning, argument, logic, thought: it is spontaneously available, thoroughly recognizable, widely shared. It *feels*, indeed, as if it has always been there."[20] The commonsense representation of a young Black girl as a highly intelligent and noble, vampiric savage maintains the "cultural script that has been handed down over the generations ... that *some children are more innocent than others, and Black children are not innocent at all.*"[21] This narrative not only reinforces Hollywood's unspoken colorblind commitments to making white people (especially white women) the heroine even at the end of the world but also further highlights the suspiciously racist switch of Melanie from white to Black. It was not random or happenstance; it was "commonsense."

All the Gifts This Girl Has

At the end of the world, Black girls like Melanie are imbued with white fear and angst for the future. They represent the looming inability for white people to dream, to imagine, and to create. They encourage white selfishness and cruelty; it is Black children who make white people once happy and caring like Justineau into vectors of despair and hopelessness. Even in a world where everyone is white except her, Melanie holds the reins for the future and either represents hope (as an experiment that can help cure us all) or misery (the one thing that has destroyed what we thought the future could look like).

While the book's Melanie rejects and wants to dispose of her name for the Grecian beauty, Pandora, the film uses Pandora's story as an inferential note to position Melanie as both a marker of change and of dystopia. We are supposed to see Melanie not as a Black girl who spends more than half of the film in restraints, eating maggots and cats, growling at people, yet scared of what others can do to her, all while naively loving and supporting her captors. We are not supposed to see Melanie as the one needing freedom, love, or care, when there are white people (especially white women) to keep safe. We are not supposed to recognize Melanie's ability to choose the future she wants, which is advantageous for her and the world that she imagines, as the proper use of her "gifts" as part human and part hungry. We are, like Justineau, supposed to be sad, despondent, and even angry that this Black girl would ruin the world and our future with it.

However, Melanie shirks this role. Rather than living the rest of her life in fear, obscurity, and only able to eat and experience new things at the behest of (fairer) others, Melanie makes a choice. Melanie sees her decision as a shift toward opportunity, worldmaking, and a life that perhaps looks different than her captors have imagined, but a life that supports her growth and desire for learning and beauty. After she sees children like her who are living in community, learning with each other, and living uncaged from others' expectations or feelings, Melanie liberates herself. She realizes that the world her captors have promised her is not the one that she wants. She learns that people like her can exist fully formed and full without the presence of guns, violence, or fear. Her gifts are those that she can harness for herself and manifest her own future. She understands that her future is her own to mold, and to create it, she must use her gifts differently than how she was trained. Melanie ultimately learns that she need not change her name. By embracing herself, her gifts, and the future she imagines is possible through her own world-making, she becomes Pandora.

When the Waters Rise: Black Girls as Levees

Unlike Melanie, we begin to see a world at its natural end through a Black girl's eyes in *Beasts of the Southern Wild*. Adapted from Lucy Alibar's play *Juicy and Delicious*, the critically acclaimed film *Beasts of the Southern Wild* is also about a salvific Black girl who despite violence, squalor, and abandonment, saves her community from complete ruin. *Beasts* centers the experiences of a six-year-old Black girl, Hushpuppy (Quvenzhané Wallis), and her curiosity about life, animals, and love. Hushpuppy lives in a makeshift trailer a few yards from her father's trailer, in a community beyond the levees of New Orleans called the Bathtub. The community is full of people living beyond the reaches of the government, taxes, or traditional jobs who thrive through communal gatherings, trade, and by feeding themselves from nature's bounty.[22] Despite the makeshift community they have created, the fierce sense of loyalty to the Bathtub and to rejecting the norms and beliefs of the hegemonic community behind the levees characterizes Hushpuppy's rearing.

Hushpuppy's major conflict occurs between herself and her father (Dwight Henry); Wink, as her father is called, disappears for multiple days then returns in a hospital gown and bracelet. Despite his disappearance and Hushpuppy's repeated statement that she wants to go to his house, he yells at her and tells her to go away. He refuses to hear or see her need to understand what is going on, so she sets her house on fire. This interaction between father and daughter ultimately causes Hushpuppy to believe she "broke something"—visualized through a major storm that washes away and displaces much of their community and produces the fantastical images of glacier chunks breaking off. The broken glaciers allow the release of enormous horned boars, supposedly the beasts of the film's title, that go on to track Hushpuppy and her community's "weak hearts" as she describes them.

Throughout the film, Hushpuppy takes a narrator role, commenting on the ways of the Bathtub. The people are always celebratory, with "more holidays than the rest of the world," because they understand how to be in community with the land and with each other. Sharing fresh caught seafood, beer, and childrearing responsibilities, the people of the Bathtub are "who the Earth is for."[23] Hushpuppy's narration feels more pressing, omniscient, and omnipresent than a typical six-year-old's does. This morphing from narrator to character and back to narrator presents Hushpuppy as all-knowing and, in some ways, lends to a reading of her character as genderless (and sometimes masculine) and older than a child, as is prevalent in critical commentary about the film. Because she is mostly dirty, without pants, and living in her own space, critics read her as "gender fluid." Because she lives in her own house, critics read her as "self-sufficient" and "aristocratic." And, because she is Black, critics read Hushpuppy as "preternaturally alert" and therefore an appropriate receptacle of violence.[24]

Hushpuppy is transformed into a Black girl in the play's adaptation to the screen because Black girls are routinely read as adults, or masculine, and therefore do not require help or support. She also has had to become self-sufficient and yet—as a six-year-old Black girl—is a more appropriate visual receptacle of violence to the screenwriter and director who recast the play's protagonist from an eleven-year-old white boy (whom the playwright describes as "a sweet little Southern boy. Not the sharpest knife in the box") to the Hushpuppy we come to know.[25] As bell hooks explains in her gloriously sharp review of the film, "For Hushpuppy and those like her, there is no love, no hands holding on, just a blank emptiness onto which any mark can be placed, any fantastical story written" because like *The Girl with All the Gifts*, *Beasts of the Southern Wild* tells all of us that Black girls do not need love, affection, or care.[26] They are simply supposed to save the world so that everyone else can benefit.

Receptacles of Violence: Black Girls on Screen

The director explains the change from raceless "sweet Southern boy" to girl happened because they changed the screenplay to fit the actors they cast and found Quvenzhané Wallis to be "incredibly wise and strong. . . . That's what this whole movie is about: this moral girl who believes in right and wrong so strongly, and has this fierceness and sweetness that are sitting inside her at the same time. That very much comes from Quvenzhané. That's who she is."[27] The original play illustrates some tenderness, intimacy, and openness between the boy and his father. Hushpuppy is given the opportunity to hear and see evidence of his father's prognosis. Then when Daddy randomly asks, "Could you touch me? I can't remember the last touch someone touched me that wasn't them trying to stop me from knocking their teeth out or setting them on fire," Hushpuppy gets an indication of love, care, and vulnerability.[28] He learns that a tough man like Daddy could desire touch, the kind made from tenderness and care, even from him. It is alarming that the boy doesn't know how, yet he musters some version of touch through a punch in the arm. Daddy appreciates this touch and says, "That's good. You're such a sweet, stupid little booger."[29] This interaction between them bespeaks a loving intimacy between father and child. Hushpuppy knows and is known for sweetness.

Hushpuppy also experiences care and tenderness through others in his life. When the boy is feeling lonely and confused, he can speak with and engage his mother's ghost in cat food, flowers, and nice words. She is always present, even if not in physical form. Even the schoolteacher, Miss Bathsheba, speaks and engages in sweetness, despite the otherwise problematic ideas expressed by her and others in the text (namely, racism, homophobia, ableism, and the general encouragement of violence). Between Hushpuppy and other children, there's an appreciation of tenderness and love, even though he is presented as a "stupid" child. These factors do not impact Hushpuppy's or others' ability to embrace love, sweetness, and care. This intentional intimacy and tenderness is not present for the eponymous Hushpuppy in the film. Because the screenwriter and director specifically rewrote the script with a Black girl embodying Hushpuppy speaks volumes about the cultural attitudes that shape who is worthy of care and support and who is not.

Throughout the film, Hushpuppy is left alone. Read as independent and self-sufficient, Hushpuppy rarely experiences support and care. Unlike her patronym, Hushpuppy's relationship with her father is generally contentious and without intimacy. He regularly speaks to her in a tone that is violent and accusatory. He regularly pulls, pushes, slaps, and grabs her. He disappears for days and is seemingly more concerned with his friends and their demise than his daughter's. This is a problematic representation not only of Black fatherhood but of the type of child who is deserving of mistreatment. Hushpuppy only begins to experience intimacy and care with her father after he is sick and unable to fend for himself.

Although he refuses to give her any information about his condition, she learns he is not well; she only learns the fullness of her father's condition when he is days away from dying. In the scene where Daddy finally tells her he is sick, and she begins to cry, he finally allows her close enough to him that she falls asleep with his arm wrapped around her. This one intimate and caring moment between them is preceded by him marking his part of the house separate from hers, with rules like "no toys, no girl stuff over here" animating his movements.[30] She learns that even when she is present, the things she enjoys should be concealed. She must navigate the world always assessing the needs and desires of others who make the rules. This scene does not exist in the play.

In the film, Hushpuppy's conjuring of her mother only occurs when she is without food or supervision for days. Rather than a ghostly apparition that brings comfort in difficult times, Hushpuppy's mother (or more accurately Hushpuppy calling out to her) marks some of the most turbulent moments when Hushpuppy feels the world is spiraling out of control. In several scenes throughout the film, she yells out to her mother saying, "Momma, I think I broke something!"[31] This phrasing and calling out to her mother as the aurochs (boars) emerge from glaciers reveal Hushpuppy's belief that she is the cause for all the bad things that have happened. Because Daddy told her, "The first time she looked at me, it made her heart beat so big, that she thought it would blow up. That's why she swam away," she believes she caused her mother to leave.[32]

Later, during an argument in which he chastises her for "having to worry about [her] all the time," she says defiantly, "I hope you die. And after you die, I'll go to your grave and eat birthday cake all by myself."[33] In response, Daddy falls to the ground, has a seizure, and is unresponsive. This is another instance where Hushpuppy learns that care and affection only come from her; when she is engaging with animals, with other people, and with herself, she operates with love, understanding, and intentionality. Everyone else who is supposed to care for her, even her teacher at school, operates with aloofness or disdain. However, when she challenges this treatment, she learns that only negative experiences follow.

This cause and effect throughout the film, either in the narratives that Hushpuppy is told or in the one she espouses about the world and the "scientists who will study [her] in the future," encourages her to believe that she has otherworldly power.[34] She alone can shape all the negative things that happen in the world with just the utterance of her mouth. While this is in line with the power that her mother had to make water boil just by walking by it, per Daddy's folklore about her, Hushpuppy's associated belief in her own negativity only works because she is a Black girl that lives outside of the societal parameters set for Black girls. Because she simply came into the world, her mother left her. Because she is not dainty, friendly, or overtly feminine, Hushpuppy deserves to be yelled at and slapped around. Because she speaks up and speaks out, her world reflects the negative things that society believes Black girls should have. Whereas the white boy Hushpuppy is associated with being dim-witted and therefore sweet and caring, Black girl Hushpuppy is smart enough to conjure her father's demise and self-sufficient enough to need no care or affection from anyone. This juxtaposition throughout the film, and in comparison to the play, is only reified by her so-called genderless presentation.

Are Black Girls Genderless?

In more than half of the film, Hushpuppy is not wearing pants; her dingy white shirt and orange underwear are even represented in the promo of the film. Her hair is uncombed. She lives among animals and does not wash regularly. She eats cat food and plays in mud, when left to her own imagination. Hushpuppy is regularly called "the man" and chastised for crying, for caring, for "girl stuff." When members of the Bathtub are taken to a government-run disaster relief shelter after Hushpuppy "broke something," she is put in a blue dress with embroidered flowers, her hair braided back and away from her face; while the other kids play and laugh, she stares blankly at her father being hooked up to medical equipment (the first real recognition in the film that he is ill).[35] The audience is supposed to read this as the domestication of the "wild beasts" that live in the Bathtub, and yet we anticipate the escape that she and her community members make. We know that this isn't right. However, the scene speaks volumes about the ways gender is read onto Black girls and their bodies (especially poor Black girls), not only in the ways the script is written but also in how Hushpuppy's freedom or containment is represented by specific markers of dress and decorum.

As early as age four, girls are taught the parameters of gender; they learn what things they can say or do, whether they can play and with whom, and how to interact with adults based on their perceived gender.[36] For Black girls, like those I mention in earlier chapters, girlhood is marked by rules, judgment, and violence. Black girls like Hushpuppy are taught that they do not deserve protection or care and that they must sustain themselves regardless of who their guardians are. Hushpuppy knows that her doing "girl stuff" is not allowed near her father and that "girl stuff" includes crying and being vulnerable. She learns that she must fend for herself, even against those who are supposed to protect and care for her. She also learns that they can leave her at any time. We see throughout the film that others fail her, even though she is supposed to always be there, always be present, always be caring for them. When she calls out to her mother, she receives no answer. When she goes looking for her, she is told that she cannot stay. Her community within the Bathtub and even the government officials who attempt to rescue them recognize her girlness, and yet critics regularly remark that she is "androgenous," "gender fluid," or "genderless." Because if Hushpuppy is not a girl, her self-sufficiency, her ability to speak up, her sense of adventure, her love of all animals and people, her desire for care and concern can be written off as if she is an "aristocrat" and "not a little girl you need to indulge with a bored sigh."[37] Indeed, if Hushpuppy is not a girl "you need to indulge" at all as white critics claim, we do not need to concern ourselves with the violence, the abandonment, or the structural and communal problems that allow a six-year-old Black girl to live by herself and eat cat food. There is no need to recognize the biases that keep Black girls outside of girlhood, until they are being so-called rescued by the State and made into the white liberal ideal of girlhood represented by Hushpuppy's French-braided hair and collared dress. We need not acknowledge the failure of everyone involved, including the problematic screenwriter and director as well as the critics, Academy, and larger society who envisioned and celebrated this fantastical hellscape brought to life by a Black girl.

Berated, abused, abandoned, and forgotten, Hushpuppy creates the film's triumph. It is her adventure, care, and love that allows her father to transition in peace. It is her ingenuity and vision that creates a path forward for her community in the Bathtub. Hushpuppy saves the day when she decides to care for herself first.

Black Girls at the End of the World

Although they are two characters created to be white, experiencing the end of the world and the beginning of a new one through the vantage point of white directors and writers, both Hushpuppy and Melanie are Black girls creating futures for themselves and those for whom they care. Both films, *The Girl with All the Gifts* and *Beasts of the Southern Wild*, illustrate the ways that cinematic representations of Black girls encourage the problematic treatment of Black girls in service of white peoples' needs and desires to process their own racism, trauma, and response to the environment. They further support the loss of subjectivity for Black girls, who rather than being supported, loved, and protected are pushed out of childhood to justify the violence they experience. These Black girls are overly burdened with heroism for the sake of white people. Black girls like Melanie and Hushpuppy are imbued with racist language about Black girls' capabilities due to their lack of proximity to whiteness.

By resisting their containment, Melanie and Hushpuppy provide a different way to understand Black girls' subjectivities beyond the silver screen. Within derelict landscapes and alongside others' feelings of despair, Melanie and Hushpuppy are inventive, creative, and forthright. With care and love, they help others transition and accept death. Using intelligence and ingenuity, they plan and develop paths forward for the living. Melanie and Hushpuppy illustrate how Black girls in the everyday are working against the people and structures that actively dehumanize and disrespect them, yet constantly beg for their sacrifice. Black girls like Little Miss Flint know and resist these problematic distortions of their abilities, working against and alongside these ideas to create space for themselves and the futures they wish to live in. As Hushpuppy says repeatedly, Black girls know who they are and what their place is within this universe. They know what we are still trying to figure out. At the end of the world, will you listen to them?

CHAPTER 5

Dispensable Black Girls

Throw Them All Away!

> I promised that I wouldn't stuff her, my girl self, into my girdles and the other undergarments that make me fit for the world we live in. I promised to carry my girl self on my shoulders and celebrate her. In this way, I am acknowledging the ways she has been a warrior and protector of my sanity.
> —DaMaris B. Hill, *Breath Better Spent*

Historically in the US, Black girls' value was determined by whether they could maintain a household, grow/harvest agricultural commodities, and live out their reproductive potential. Within their communities, whether they were educated, marriageable, or even beautiful was constructed by their fathers, uncles, brothers, and suitors based on so-called scientific information such as the spread of their hips, the thickness of their ankles, and their ability to carry weight. The inability to carry out wifely duties (which included bearing boy children and pleasing their husbands in whatever way they wanted) was enough to nullify any marriage, leaving Black girls destitute so their suitors could find someone more worthy of patriarchal protection and therefore value. This value system meant that the worse thing a girl could be was useless (literally without use); she must find a way to illustrate her value, even if the structures to identify value left her without community or personal choice.

Today's culture might call these girls "pick mes"—a play on the word "pickney"/"pickaninny," meaning a Black child—which describes girls and women who actively promote and support patriarchal values and violence only to encourage a man to choose them for marriage and therefore protect their own value, proving their usefulness.[1] Whereas the particularities of their decisions are individual, the system through which Black girls learn their value is made clear through the narratives of Black girls as fast, the conduit of men's emotional evolution, and as invisible-hypervisible fodder for entertainment. When their value is no longer needed or deemed worthy within the system of patriarchy, Black girls are rendered expendable.

Kindred to the role of salvific Black girls whose value is determined by the protection they can create for others—I now turn to the Black girls whose narratives communicate their value in their disposability. Disposable Black girls can often be identified in the need for their narratives to deal with chaos, loss, and fear, and being faced with Black men who are willing to dispose of them eagerly because they are not behaving how they want. Extending the fuckboy-to-fatherhood evolution to larger constructions of Black masculinity that are built on the demonization of Black girls and their needs, these narratives further digital Black feminism scholar Catherine Knight Steele's astute assertion that "Black womanhood has always been profitable for someone."[2] The characters who lead the films *Project Power* and *A Wrinkle in Time* illustrate how Black girls' safety measures are regarded as disrespectful and a justification for their mistreatment. Robin and Meg, girls struggling to create a sense of normalcy while losing parents, friends, and safety, show us the difficulty Black girls face to protect themselves from the very people who are supposed to protect them. They are dispensable when they go against ideologies of Black masculinity that encourage selfishness, self-centered decision-making, and the failure of others to protect them. Their value is nullified, and they become disposable, when they refuse to be "pick mes" and no longer serve patriarchal cultures that encourage a focus on the needs of men rather than the Black girls who need our protection.

Real Fantastical Lies

Much like the construction of the white savior film due to Hollywood's allegiance to colorblind racial ideologies that I discuss alongside the Black girl saviors, *Project Power* and *A Wrinkle in Time*, and other films in the same genre with disposable Black girls, capture what I call fantastical realism—cinematic worlds like the one we currently live in but with elements of fantastical experiences. The genre relies on the audience to recognize and assume the tenets of the film without further explanation. The construction of injustice is always presented as typical and therefore commonsense, yet the fantastical elements are usually attributed to white people or men. This juxtaposition reasserts creatives' lack of imagination (what Ebony Elizabeth Thomas calls "the imagination gap") in their creation of cinematic representations that refuse to render women and girls of color in nonstereotypical ways.[3] Whereas *Project Power* is an original screenplay by Mattson Tomlin, *A Wrinkle in Time*'s content is based on the previous film and book. Regardless of the origins, both films present Black girls as disposable because of choices they have made; Black girls are rendered unvaluable because of what their lives required of them. Other characters in both films change, shift, move, imagine, and live differently even after they make terrible choices. Black girls, however, are not given those options.

The lie of realism then appears when we assume that injustice and violence as it occurs on screen is justifiable and commonsense. In *Feminist Theory: From Margin to Center*, feminist cultural critic bell hooks contends that the structural dichotomy of care and violence in the US rests on the idea that violence is justifiable especially when enacted upon the powerless.[4] I add that violence, on screen, solidifies the justification for violence in the everyday and that that violence is justifiable based on who is being violated. In *Project Power* and *A Wrinkle in Time*, as well as every other example I provide in this book, Black girls are always already justified targets of violence. Historian Treva Lindsey describes this as the ideology of "Black violability"—the idea that Black people are always violable but also that Black girls, women, transpeople, and gender nonbinary folk are justified targets.[5] This means then that (1) these people are seen as typical and therefore invisible victims of violence, that (2) they/we look like the kinds of people who are violent or cause the violence that we experience and therefore deserve it, and that (3) we "make sense" as the victims of murder and maiming as well as mental and emotional violence, making others the so-called true victims who must be protected. The violence inflicted upon us is hence victimless, justifiable, and unremarkable. African American literary expert Erica Edwards explains that

> Black women captives on the home front—on the plantation, on the chain gain, in the prison yard or solitary cell, in the car, in the front-yard garden, at the airport, on the sidewalk—served as test cases for the techniques of surveillance and torture that would be exported after 2001. . . . What they called the war on terror, what they had previously called the war for democracy, was the war of conquest. This country has never ceased its drumbeat of war. It has never faltered in its quest to penetrate, castigate, and domesticate Black female flesh. But neither has it been so brazen in its recruitment of Black women to hold its drumsticks.[6]

In as much as Black women have served as the "test cases" of white supremacist violence as well as the drum majors for US imperial "techniques of surveillance and torture," I find that Black girls face these cultures of violence in person and on screen. The shared beliefs within and beyond Black cultural practices that encourage misogynoir legitimate Black girls' experiences of violence with silver screen cultural productions that present Black girls as the only acceptable targets of violence, whether perpetuated by Black people or by others.

As the only legitimate targets of violence, Black girls are represented in *Project Power* and *A Wrinkle in Time* as disposable. Once the other characters construct a future for themselves, using the

Black girl characters around them to bolster their confidence and strategize their freedom, Black girls are left to fend for themselves. Despite being violently handled or emotionally abused, Robin and Meg illustrate how Black girls learn to protect themselves, help others, and craft a just world where fantastical things can happen. Like the Black girls I discuss in other chapters, Robin and Meg refute disposability through creativity, refusing the very characterization that they are supposed to fit.

"They Took Somethin' from Me": *Project Power*'s Disposable Sidekick

A new drug wreaks havoc in New Orleans. The buyers, sellers, and law enforcement note that the highly coveted and expensive drug—a small vial called "power"—gives any user superhuman abilities where they can run, jump, punch, and move like superheroes. Within four minutes of the film's start, this premise comes to bear when Robin (Dominique Fishback) attempts to sell the drug to three boys who brutally attack her to steal her bag. A police officer (Joseph-Gordon Levitt) shows up and pretends to handcuff her, letting the boys walk free even after assaulting her, communicating that the sale of drugs is a higher offense than the beating of an unarmed Black girl. Shortly after, the officer pays her for the confiscated vial and gives her a previously impounded motorcycle for her belated birthday; the audience learns that her arrest was a ruse, and they know each other. Despite their friendship, within five minutes of *Project Power* starting, audiences are exposed to a brutal physical attack on a Black girl that goes unanswered beyond Levitt's character, Frank, asking if she's okay. She answers by saying, "I had it."[7]

Robin's abuse continues throughout the film, perpetuated by every man she encounters. She is repeatedly talked to aggressively, grabbed, yelled at, pushed, and pulled. Multiple men, including Jamie Foxx's character "the Major," kidnap her, forcing her to cry, cower, and scream for help. However, no one ever comes to her aid. The film is propelled by a friendship that forms between Robin and the Major, the same person who kidnapped her, threw her in a trunk, and yelled at her until she complied. He repeatedly threatens her life and her mother's, saying at one point:

> I know you scared. I know you feeling like fight or flight, but I'ma tell you right now, you just breathe and get through it because listen, you don't know who I am and what I'm about, but I got to find that source [of the drug supply]. I need to get to the top of the food chain. But you keep messing around with me and acting like you don't know shit, I'ma knock your ass out and then I'm gonna go kill your mother. I'ma kill Irene. Look me in my eyes, am I lying?[8]

The audience is supposed to feel for Robin, but only to the extent that kidnapping is traumatic. We are supposed to think that the Major's tactics are necessary and therefore justified. This is how all interactions of violence are manifested in the film. For example, the white man teacher who confronts Robin in the only school scene in the film, wherein she is texting to locate her cousin who is missing while in class, says: "I know you don't think this stuff is serious, you don't think it's important, but it is. Right now, you're getting a D in this class, Robin. It's an easy class. . . . So since you don't seem to be worried about your grades or graduating, you must have a plan, right? So, what is that plan, Miss Reilly?"[9] Beyond the problematic shaming of her by publicly discussing her grade in class and calling the class "easy" to suggest she is cognitively unable to do the work, the idea that Robin is never serious and never aware of the problems surrounding her is repeated throughout the film. The vantage point of others around her, particularly Black and white men, is that Robin has no sense of her actions, has no ability to assess situations, and is not savvy enough to understand the veneers used in communication with her. Her musical talent is explained as a foil to "true" power or understanding. In their words, she couldn't possibly be smart enough to understand because she's a rapper.

Black Patriarchy as White Liberal Sentiments: Questioning Robin's Power

Her love for music and talent as a rapper is used as a salve several times, pushing the audience to identify more with the musical resonances than the words that are being said. Her talent too is supposed to illustrate her resilience, as if her commitment to her skill absolves the other people from the violent ways they interact with her, or the regular commentary about how the government has failed Black women, Black people, and New Orleans. Despite her constantly screaming for help, the answer is more physical violence and threats. She is supposed to plan herself out of systemic neglect and violence; the Major says as much when he confronts her about selling power to addicts. After she finishes patching his wounds from an earlier fight, he asks why she's dealing rather than getting good grades. When she reveals that her mother has diabetes and needs surgery, and thus they need money, he tells her:

> THE MAJOR: That's easy. Go to the army.
> ROBIN: [She scoffs.] So what it don't trip you up killing fools?
> TM: Yeah it tripped me up. But that was my skillset. And what the system do? It took advantage of me. But I know now I gotta work the system harder than it's working me. That's what you gotta do. You're young, you're Black, you're a woman. The system is designed to swallow you whole. You gotta find out what you do better than anybody else and rock that. So what you gon do? Hmm? How you gon leave your mark?
> R: [She replies almost annoyed.] I rap.[10]

In response, he laughs. His laughter communicates again how rapping is not "serious" or a real contribution to the society on which he says she should leave her mark. Because he has figured out how to use his skillset of violence and murder to "work the system harder than it's working" him, he chastises Robin for her focus on her mother and their familial needs. While selling drugs and rapping is an easy target for the liberal individualized argument for why Black children are doing the wrong thing, going to the army is a response that is easily thrown at Black children in many neglected communities like those shown in the film. Their conversation, one between a Black girl and a Black man, seems to mirror neoliberal arguments rather than a specificity of Robin's experience or even the Major's.

This is one of the numerous instances where the heavy hand of the all-white male writing, production, and directional team make their political beliefs known; the Major, rather than the white male cop Frank who constantly proclaims his commitment to the city of New Orleans (which the audience is supposed to interpret as his commitment to Black people), becomes the speaker for white supremacist beliefs about Black inferiority and how to make oneself useful and therefore worthy of protection. His faux Black conservatism, illustrated in the conversation with Robin, communicates the opposite of what his own experience would foretell. He joined the military and was great at killing people, yet they experimented on him to make him even better at it; after he is discharged, they kidnap his daughter, and his experimentation has destroyed his mental faculties to the point that he has visions and loses consciousness regularly. And despite these experiences, his response to a Black girl—one who resembles his daughter—who says she is struggling to contribute financially to her family as well as cope with the death of her father, is to join the same military that mistreated and abused him to illustrate her power.

Rather than listening to her experience and understanding it as a Black man, and the father of a Black daughter, he explains to Robin her own experience, "You're young, you're Black, you're a woman. The system is designed to swallow you whole."[11] These statements among others in the film standout because he explains how she should see the system working itself on her, as if she has not already seen and experienced this swallowing firsthand. His response is taken directly from liberal talking points about the plight of Black America and how Black people just need to work harder to assimilate ("get good grades and stay in school") despite the system consistently disenfranchising them, using them as test subjects for pharmaceutical drugs and experiments, and discounting the real ways the system works to use and then dispose of Black people on every level. Spoken from a Black man to a Black girl, this phrasing morphs from white liberal belief into benevolent misogynoir.

The Major communicates his disapproval in a patriarchal tone, reframing Robin's experience of misogynoir with her teacher in an earlier scene as a lack of fatherly attention and structure. When her response to his question about her power is rap, he pushes her antagonistically: "What you gon be the next Cardi B? Huh? Cardi C?"; "How you gon be a rapper if you got stage fright?"; "If you whack, just say you whack."[12] These statements not only downplay the real cultural work that rappers do, especially given the example of Cardi B who is contemporarily one of the most publicly active political rap figures, but they also cheapen the political possibilities for people who decide to pursue rap music as their "power."[13] Even after she performs for him, he says, "You good, damn good. [She smirks.] That's your power. You take that, you leverage that, you use your power to take the system down."[14] Again, the use of the Major to communicate his approval (and the audience's) of her skill has a patriarchal stamp of importance; now that she has stood up to his antagonisms and illustrated that she does have talent, she's worthy of pursuing her musical dreams.

Plus size and nonbinary Black woman rapper Chika is the author of all of Robin's lyrics throughout the film, and the ways that she as rapper has been castigated for not conforming to traditional femme aesthetics within the rap world seems to also be approved by the Major's statements. Ultimately, Black girls' skills are framed as a power that should be used to work within the system that not only "swallows" them but also blames them for the swallowing. Even when they illustrate adept skill or traditional academic knowledge, the jokes are always on them. As the Major says to Robin after she offers an explanation as to why his daughter might have powers based on the testing he experienced, "Oh, okay. Yeah, you hood, but you smart huh," communicating that even when she does apply her school aptitude, it is joke worthy.[15]

Despite her talent and intellect, Robin's disposability is pervasive in all interactions. The second half of the film is riddled with instances where other people decide whether Robin is useful or not. She hears from various sources that she is only important when she is useful, and the moment she is not, she's harmed. The Major reminds her, "We ain't no Batman and Robin, that's a movie, this is real life," though he constantly needs and accepts her help.[16]

Officer Frank takes a similar stance when he wants information from her but would rather assert authority over her than listen. In a conversation about the Major's whereabouts, Frank berates Robin for her compliance:

> ROBIN: Why is he a bad guy? Because he's done some bad things? What about you? You do bad things too!
> FRANK: That is almost a good point, but the bad things I have done—
> R: He's just looking for his daughter. Everything he's doing, he's doing it for her. That sound like a bad guy to you?
> F: That's what he told you?
> R: That's what I know.
> F: Look, I'm sorry that you miss your dad.
> R: Don't do me like that.
> F: But this guy is telling you a story. [Robin rolls her eyes.] He's not here looking for his daughter. He's setting up shop.
> R: [She laughs.] So you think he's the source of power?
> F: Yes.
> R: Well he's not. He's trying to stop it.[17]

Whereas Robin has spent twenty-four hours getting to know the Major, assessing his motivations, and helping him locate new leads in his search to locate his daughter, Frank's assignment is new, and the information he has is wrong. Yet when Robin explains herself and asserts her own assessments of the situation and the Major (and Frank), he brings up "missing her dad" as an excuse for her decision to support the Major's mission. Oddly enough, the Major doubles down on this line a few minutes later when Robin tries to convince him to work with Frank. He says, "Do I look like your daddy or sumthin?"[18] The contrasted use of patriarchal power then chastisement for seeking or following it further illustrates how Robin's life is useful for others but then used against her when she asserts herself. They both use her for their own ends, but then position her motivations as misplaced—a vestige of her love for her father rather than her ability to determine the best outcome in the situation. Both Frank and the Major give more pushback to Robin asserting herself than they ever give each other, yet Robin helps them both survive. Furthermore, her own survival is only approximate to the other Black girl in the film, the Major's daughter, Tracy (Kyanna Simpson).

Survival of the Fittest: Black Girls in Contrast

Aside from most antagonistic characters being white (women), the film positions Robin and Tracy as two sides of the same Black girl coin. Whereas Robin is fatherless, a drug dealer, and living in the "hood" in New Orleans, Tracy is positioned as her opposite—smart, childlike, powerful, and worthy of being saved by her doting father. Robin is worldly and able to handle things herself, while Tracy is shown (for the first time outside of her father's visions) completing a puzzle; Robin works while Tracy plays. Robin's father's passing is not given context other than how his love of music narrated their lives and how he encouraged Robin's musical talent; Tracy's father, the Major who becomes "Art" (a nickname that humanizes him beyond authoritarian military rhetoric), on the other hand gives her the power to create, renew, and change life forms. Her blood and spinal fluid are what is being used to fuel the drug that Robin sells on the street; while Tracy's body gives life, Robin's work takes it. Tracy is a modern-day Henrietta Lacks, as explained by the doctor who creates the drug, providing an "evolution" that will shift science for millennia. Although Tracy does not get to respond or even narrate her own experiences at the hands of the doctor, her father and protector, the Major, refuses this usefulness of his daughter even while using Robin similarly. It is not clear how old Tracy is or whether her power is only that which is of use to others, but when the Major's visions collapse Robin and Tracy into one, such that Robin is Tracy, Robin becomes worthy of protection because Tracy matters to him.

This collapsing of Robin and Tracy falls apart when Tracy has been rescued, yet Robin has been captured. The captors are willing to exchange one Black girl for another, communicating not only that there's a value system in which there's a determination of which Black girls are worthy of being protected but also that others should recognize which Black girl is valuable and which is not. To others, Robin's usefulness is only in her exchange for (or rescue of) Tracy, who can both destroy and heal. They share the power to destroy and heal, however.

Robin's musical talent, her medical skills, her intelligence, her ability to assess people and situations, and her care for people and animals are derided. But they are the characteristics that make her as valuable as Tracy. While others are fighting and trying to communicate their powers, it is Robin who not only helps them but also locates and rescues Tracy. She recognizes her, even though she has never seen her. She comforts her, although she herself is scared. She frees everyone else so that they can escape, yet there is a short instance where all the characters question whether Robin is worthy of being saved, too. The Major determines that she is, even while Tracy believes that Robin cannot be saved. The Major decides to take a power pill:

> TRACY: No Daddy. You know what'll happen if you do that.
> DOCTOR: I will kill her, Arthur, right now, right in front of you.
> THE MAJOR: [To Tracy] I love you more than anything in the world, you hear me? I love you, but there's no way we're leaving her behind. [They hug.][19]

While Tracy's rescue hinges on every other murder that happens in the film in order for the Major to get to her, Robin's requires the Major to sacrifice himself. This reversal of him being her captor to being her savior transforms his kidnapping of her, his chastisement of her talent, and his use of her for his own ends into a patriarchal sacrifice. The Major is willing to let go of the thing he truly loves (his daughter), to not leave a soldier behind. The conversation between the Major and Robin (as she is being threatened with death by the doctor) communicates her value and therefore his sacrifice.

> THE MAJOR: Robin you alright?
> DOCTOR: Don't talk to her!
> THE MAJOR: Let me tell you something, Robin. You did a great job. You saved my daughter's life.[20]

Robin's "job" makes her deserving of his sacrifice, even as his statement further highlights who is actually important. Tracy was saved; therefore, Robin can be too. The two Black girls together then save the Major after he uses his power, solidifying their usefulness to him and each other.

The final exchange between the Major and Robin brings his patriarchal influence more clearly into view. As Tracy sits in a truck waiting to leave, the Major says his goodbyes.

> FRANK: Let me ask you something. You think this is really over?
> THE MAJOR: For me it is. [They shake hands.] It's time to jet.
> TM: [To Robin] Hey, you. Go to my truck. [Hands over keys.] Make sure you check the trunk. You remember what I said? [She nods; he hugs her; she is expressionless.] There's something great inside of you Robin. Use it. [He kisses her on the head; she pulls away and nods visibly sad.][21]

While missing her father is regularly used against her as a reason for her mistreatment, the Major becomes a pseudofather when he sacrifices himself for her. Although they have never touched or hugged, the Major's final directive to Robin is structured around his physical touch. They are not Batman and Robin nor are they father and daughter, yet the Major again reminds her of her need to "use her power," accentuating this statement with a kiss on her head—a gesture typical of Hollywood interactions between fathers and children or intimate partners. Oddly, this affectionate exchange feels latently erotic compared to one between Robin and her mother; through the "streetwise" framing of Robin as sidekick, especially against the backdrop of Tracy playing with a puzzle and being rescued, Robin is aged up. Without the school scene earlier in the movie, and the Major's constant barrage of questions about her motivations and her contributions, Robin operates as an adult among adults.

The film communicates repeatedly that Robin's usability and lack of care for school makes her an adult: she is not coddled or talked to with care, except by her mother; she is not worthy of rescue; she is a helper and is valuable to others who might make use of her. Robin is kidnapped, locked in a moving freight trailer, hit, and threatened several times so that Tracy and the Major could be reunited. Her usefulness overrides any affection or purpose she might determine on her own. Even when she finally returns home after what seems like several days (though treated as one long day in the film), her mother never asks where she was or where the money she piles on the bed came from. She simply holds the can of soup Robin gave her, hugs her with a confused face, and says, "I love you too."[22] Robin's consolation for everything that she has been through is soup for her mother and money for her mother's surgery. Both of which only illuminate her usefulness to her mother.

Although Robin is consistently displayed as the disposable, violable character throughout *Project Power*, she also manifests a different reality for herself based on her own needs, determinations, and beliefs. The film begins with her motivation to make a future for herself and her mother possible through making money and music. The film ends with her providing the future that she desires—her song is played on the radio and her mother has the money for surgery. The song manifests through her exchanges with the Major; she realizes she has the skill and confidence to create music that speaks to her experiences, her community, and her true power. Likewise, the money comes because of Robin bargaining with the Major; in exchange for helping him find Tracy, she gets $5,000 to help her mother. She claims she is charging him for "medical expenses, keeping your ass alive, kidnapping fee," which communicates her own belief in her value not only to him but to herself.[23]

Whereas Robin's ability to construct a future for herself is contingent upon her still providing for her mother and using the approval of her pseudofather to tap into her power, Meg in *A Wrinkle in Time* must go against all others to find confidence in her abilities and create a future in which both she and her family are able to exist.

Wrinkled Universes: Meg's Fantastical Takeover

Like *Beasts of the Southern Wild* and *The Girl with All the Gifts*, the film *A Wrinkle in Time* is based on a novel of the same name by Madeline L'Engle. L'Engle's *A Wrinkle in Time* was published in 1962 and follows Margaret "Meg" Murry into the multiplicity of the universe to find her father. Guided by the celestial beings Mrs. Which, Mrs. Who, and Mrs. Whatsit, Meg, her brother Charles Wallace, and her friend Calvin try to find her missing father. The novel and the first Disney made-for-TV adaptation in 2003 are fantastical imaginings of white human and nonhuman characters (save Mrs. Whatsit, who is played by Alfre Woodard in the first adaptation). However, the 2018 film follows a more multicultural framing, typical of Disney's more recent films. Whereas the book consistently refers to characters who go "white with fright" while darkness is only associated with Camazotz, the home of evil, the film casts multiple Black characters who shift the racialized dynamics of the script as well as audience interpretation of key aspects of the plot. Margaret in the book navigates the world through glasses and braces, a nervous countenance, and curly brown hair. She is perceived as stupid by her teachers for wanting to do things her own way. However, in the film Meg is awkward and suspicious, with big, coily, reddish-brown hair and purple glasses. She is a genius but has consistently underperformed since her father's disappearance. Meg becomes a child who faces bullying and self-esteem issues, a change that reflects larger discourses concerning children in 2012 rather than 1962.

Accentuated by the celebrity of media mogul–actress Oprah Winfrey and director Ava DuVernay (the pair that also brought us Keke in the show *Queen Sugar*), the 2018 adaptation follows Meg Murry (Storm Reid) who is the daughter of physicists Dr. Kate and Alex Murry. While Drs. Murry and Murry have been attempting intergalactic travel through what they call a "tesseract" or overlap in the universe's time-space continuum, Alex Murry gets lost. Four years later, Meg is dejected and depressed, as is her mother and her gifted brother, Charles Wallace. Adults around her struggle to comprehend her feelings while other children make fun of and bully her. Relying again on the audience to embrace what I call fantastical realism—a real life situation recast through fantastical elements—the decision to cast an African American girl actress as the lead in this film reshapes the many problematic statements said to Meg as those laced with misogynoir. Likewise, the characterizations of Black girls as mean, aggressive, and unassimilable metastasize the misogynoir of popular culture in this film, where a fatherless Black girl character gets bullied by a white girl, verbally mistreated by Black teachers, and called to rescue her white father from his own ambition. As I have argued elsewhere, the recasting of white characters as people of color is a hallmark of Disney's multicultural turn since the late 1990s; these changes signify attention on Disney's part to visual diversity, yet it almost always reinforces negative stereotypes of Black women and girls—choices that uphold the "magic" of Disney and misogyny toward Black girls.[24]

Meg consistently hears from her parents that she is loved. Yet, her negative feelings about herself are amplified by her bully Veronica and teachers who do nothing to prevent the vitriol she experiences. Like Robin, within minutes of the film beginning, the audience is accosted by harmful things being done and said to Meg. The fourth anniversary of her father's disappearance is marked by everyone in the local community, especially the popular girls who write a note on her locker that says: "Happy Anniversary! If only you'd disappear too," with a smiley face.[25] The girls look on with a smirk while Meg glares at them, emotionally shaken. Her bully Veronica reignites this antagonism at recess, stating, "So, looks like crazy runs in the family."

> MEG: What did you just say?
> VERONICA: I see why your dad left. [She laughs and turns around, addressing the other girls.] Who does she even think that she's talking to?
> MEG: [Nods, grabs a basketball from a girl behind her and throws it.] Hey Veronica![26]

The basketball hits Veronica in the face and she falls to the ground. Meg is sent to the office of Principal James Jenkins, a Black male teacher who was recently promoted by other teachers to lead the school. His conversation with her doubles down on the idea that Black girls' emotional needs are not as important as others, and they should refuse themselves to be better liked (and therefore better treated) in school.

> PRINCIPAL JENKINS: [Sighs] Veronica Kiley's parents are on their way here. They're worried for their daughter's safety.
> MEG: Their daughter is mean.
> PRINCIPAL: You hit her in the face. You . . . You were a top student. Top attitude. But look at you now. You . . . you're aggressive. You're hostile. You shut everybody out and then wonder why they don't like you.
> MEG: I don't wonder, and I don't care.
> PRINCIPAL: Hmm. Well . . . maybe that's your problem.
> MEG: I don't have a problem.

DISPENSABLE BLACK GIRLS

> PRINCIPAL: You can't keep using your father's disappearance as an excuse to act out. What do you think he would say about all this? Seriously, if he walked in that door today . . . what would happen?
> MEG: The world would make sense again.
> PRINCIPAL: [Sits forward, and his tone shifts from disciplinary to empathetic.] Listen. All I'm saying is, it's been four years. Odds are he's not coming back.[27]

Despite the many insults Meg has experienced over the years, Principal Jenkins sides with the bully, and seemingly the whole school, who believes that Meg's pain is not worthy of concern or respect. Her inability to focus, to be a "top student" with a "top attitude," as Principal Jenkins notes, is directly connected to her father's disappearance. Yet rather than providing a grief counselor or engaging with her emotions and how the actions of the bully provoked her, Principal Jenkins quickly hastens to describe her as "aggressive," "hostile," and defensive. Despite her resisting this characterization with "I don't have a problem," Principal Jenkins doubles down. He argues that her countenance makes people not like her, resulting in her being bullied. He also communicates that she can end her school torment by simply accepting that "he's not coming back." This exchange is magnified by the fact that the interaction occurs between a Black male principal and a Black female student.

Beyond this being a rude and disrespectful thing to say to a thirteen-year-old, the idea that Meg is the source of the hostility she experiences at school is ludicrous. His refusal to care about her mental or emotional state bespeaks a larger cultural belief about Black girls and their inability to be included. A Wrinkle in Time shows a Black man parroting white liberal ideologies of inclusion via assimilation to a Black girl child; like the Major in Project Power, Principal Jenkins stands in for the cultural misogynoir that disregards Black girls' feelings and encourages them to simply get over the traumatic things that happen to them in service of being liked and therefore accepted. Yet the girls' issue with Meg is not simply about her being liked, as evidenced by the white boy character Calvin who is quick to express his interest in Meg by complimenting her hair and remarking upon how "incredible" she is.[28] Meg does not have an issue being liked; Meg's issue is that those around her mark her as mean, aggressive, and hostile because they want her to get over things that they have not experienced.

They would rather her forget about the terrible things that she confronts every day as she mourns the loss of her father than attempt to recognize the great pain she carries into school with her. Meg's bully torments her because she is different and because the bully herself is miserable. And one would assume that as a principal and as a Black man, Principal Jenkins would recognize the faults in his own logic rather than blaming a child. However, this conversation only illuminates the tactics that Black girls face in educational environments—both those run by Black administrators and others—to push them out if they will not assimilate like white girls or Black boys do. Education researcher Monique Morris and anthropologist Savannah Shange describe the multipronged approaches used in educational environments that actively work to discount Black girls' experiences, violently chastise them for not conforming, and eventually push them out of school.[29] Even though Meg has "more potential in her pinky" than others have "in their whole body," as her brother yells across the playground, she, like Robin and other Black girls, is told to either use her power in ways that benefit others or get out.[30]

Meg's trajectory in the film, which is less physically violently than Robin's but nonetheless problematic, hinges on the assistance she receives from Mrs. Whatsit, Mrs. Who, and Mrs. Which. While Mrs. Who (Mindy Kaling) and Mrs. Which (Oprah Winfrey) seem to believe in Meg's ability to find beauty, confidence, and peace within herself, Mrs. Whatsit (Reese Witherspoon) spews negativity at Meg as regularly as she showers Charles Wallace with compliments. Every single interaction between Meg and Mrs. Whatsit is characterized by Whatsit saying rude and disrespectful things to or about Meg, arguably a representation of Meg's negative inner critic.

The first time that they are transported through the universe, via a process called "tessering," Meg lands on her back and shudders in pain. Mrs. Which encourages Mrs. Whatsit to check on Meg; she subsequently kicks her to check if she's okay.[31] This action, kicking to illustrate care, is exactly how Black girls like Meg are treated even by those who are supposed to help them.

Consistently doused in negativity or criticism, then pushed, punched, or hit to illustrate care, Black girls are treated with suspicion and irritation. Misogynoir makes this interaction and every other one between Mrs. Whatsit and Meg innocent, so much so that Mrs. Whatsit can proclaim matter-of-factly at the end of the film— once Meg has conquered IT, saved her brother, found her father, and brought light to the universe—"Well I knew you could do it all along. I never doubted you for a second."[32] It is Meg who unlocks the power of the universe, heals her self-confidence, and rescues her entire family, and yet Mrs. Whatsit is still coolly confident. Rather than her celebrating Meg's accomplishment with truth and candor, she is indifferent while Meg is graciously humble and kind. This allows the audience to accept Mrs. Whatsit's rude and violent behavior as so-called tough love, brandishing disrespectful comments and behavior as necessary acts of care for children, especially Black girls, to tap into their potential. It justifies the behavior of Principal Jenkins and Mrs. Whatsit as crucial interactions because Meg is characterized as "hostile" and "aggressive." Because Meg is "difficult," they too must be difficult to help her.

This corrosive logic also justifies IT's (the ultimate universal evil that lives on Camazotz) construction of a "better version" of Meg that distorts her imagined self. The "better" Meg does not wear glasses, has straightened hair, wears makeup and form-fitting clothes. She is "a better version of [Meg]. She's sure to be popular. Great student. Principal Jenkins is going to love her. And Calvin probably will too . . . She's perfect." The idea that a better version of Meg is perfect because she doesn't wear glasses and straightens her hair feeds a white supremacist idea about beauty and popularity that always makes coils and curls unattractive. Meg is already a great student, and she is already liked by Calvin; however, IT preys on Meg's own insecurities about her hair and her body.

Ultimately, she rejects this idea of perfection, but the societal belief about inclusion through assimilation is maintained in this characterization of so-called perfection. Black girls like Meg must conform in all aspects of their being to be accepted, not only by their romantic interests but also by other children and school administrators. This communicates that ultimately the acceptance of Black girls requires them "perfecting" themselves, reforming everything about who they are that might curl or kink to be like white girls. This idea is not new yet maintains its problematic positionality in our society. For Black girls to be accepted, they need only to give themselves up completely and be someone else. If they refuse, they are not worthy of protection, of support, of care. They are disposable and deserve the mistreatment they experience at the hands of people who are supposed to care for them. They can face evil by themselves.

Manifesting Freedom: Robin and Meg Finding Themselves

Both *Project Power* and *A Wrinkle in Time* rely on the audience's embrace of fantastical realism—plots and dialogue that use fantastical elements to accent beliefs about contemporary cultural issues. However, these films hinge on our cultural beliefs about Black girls to make the films feel real, while they extend the fantastical aspects to other characters. Robin and Meg constantly assert themselves against the abusive mistreatment they experience from teachers, parents, and other adults. Whether in New Orleans schools or white suburbia, or fantastical universes beyond them, Black girls are subject to hurtful comments rooted in stereotypes about their personalities, their expressed and hidden feelings, their family structures, and their bodies. The Black men in their lives push these narratives about them, telling them how unlikeable, how unvaluable, and how unworthy of protection they are. They are told repeatedly that their power lies in their usefulness to others' plans and liberation, rather than the talents and skills they manifest.

Despite their mistreatment, Black girls like Robin and Meg face these obstacles by locating their own inner truths about themselves and embracing the very faults that others disparage. Their real power is in manifesting the worlds they want to live in, evidenced through Meg's ability to reroute others' tessering to go where she wants to go or Robin's staunch commitment to getting what her family needs to survive regardless of others' judgment. They force time and others to bend to their will, which ultimately liberates anyone around them. The system teaches Black girls that their value renders them useless when they decide to serve themselves rather than those who fail to love and protect them. And yet, their decision to serve themselves is the realism we should recognize and reverberate.

Understanding the disposability narrative for Black girls lays a foundation to help us take seriously the characterization of Black girls as mean and aggressive. Used to dismiss the feelings of girls like Meg and Robin as an aspect of the cultural misogynoir they face, meanness and aggression are also applied to Black girls like Selah and Amy who use their forthrightness to assert themselves and make themselves known. Whereas Meg and Robin struggled to find their places within the world they lived, Selah and Amy find it and hold themselves hostage to the beliefs that others have of them. This desire for control and likeability is what motivates the Black girls in *Selah and the Spades* and *Cuties*—the subject of the next chapter.

CHAPTER 6

Mean (Black) Girls

> I know I may seem like I was being a bitch,
> but that's only because I was acting like a bitch.
> —Cady Heron, *Mean Girls* (2004)

Unlike the other films I've discussed to trace the representation of Black girls thus far, both films in this chapter are written and produced by Black women. Typically lauded for the "for us, by us" representation of Black women creating for Black consumers, cultural products created by Black women illustrate commitments and ideas that permeate Black diasporic cultures. Like DuVernay's creation of so-called fast girl Keke and anxious genius girl Meg, Black women cultural producers provide insight into how Black women perceive, understand, and often fail Black girls.

In *Buy Black: How Black Women Transformed US Pop Culture*, I explain how Black women as cultural producers influence popular culture; these artists, actresses, writers, and designers infuse their products with their experiences to not only connect with other Black women consumers but also reframe the knowledge of Black women and girls to propel popular discourses about blackness, femininity, and sexuality—a process I call "embodied objectification."[1] By bringing attention to "meanness" as a quality within Black women's cultural products that focus on Black girls, my aim here is to locate where Black girls show up within popular discourses and how Black women further structure our beliefs about who is and what is a Black girl. Like the Black fathers who position Black girls as the transformative force in their lives, I consider how Black women—through crafting stories about Black girls—create and commercialize popular narratives about Black girls being unapproachable and therefore disposable.

Recharacterizing the stereotypes of Black women as "Sapphires"—women who are angry, hostile, and generally aggressive to everyone but especially men—the Black women filmmakers in this chapter place Black girls in locations where Black people, let alone Black girls, are rarely seen or heard. In an elite private boarding high school for Selah in *Selah and the Spades* and an immigrant Muslim community in Paris for Amy in *Cuties*, Black girls become mean, aggressive, and unrepentant for wrongs done. These characters elucidate how the process of inclusion through assimilation for Black girls can corrode. In their attempts to be like other girls and rise to a level of importance rather than invisibility, Black girls become mean girls. Described in *Progressive Dystopia* as "opaque on purpose," Black girls' refusal can come in the form of "demanding to be seen but refusing to be seen through."[2] Black girl opacity then, even in so-called progressive political spaces, force others to engage the ways that they choose to be seen. This strategic negotiation occurs within Black girl ordinariness, as Savannah Shange puts it, and might be confused as meanness or aggression because Black girls do not wish to be engulfed in the process of world-making in which the State or their families participate.

While Black girls have always occupied spaces where they are seen yet unheard despite the claims that they do not exist, reframing these geographical spaces through the experiences of Black girls reshapes not only what we know about ultra-white locales but also how Black girls navigate ideas about their usefulness and their disposability.[3] *Selah and the Spades* and *Cuties* represent the advent of twenty-first-century discourses about what I call the "mean Black girl" and how fear and insecurity are presented as mean and headstrong for Black girl characters. Selah and Amy represent Black girls who have internalized ideas about them that pervade many societies. Both are darker skinned Black girls who have been described as fast, as the daughters of missing and irresponsible yet charming Black fathers, as hypervisible because of their charisma and decisiveness. And yet, they are Black girls who are disposable when they are not saving others, so they work to make themselves important. They both take on the leadership of peer groups through fear and intimidation yet experience constant anxiety about the possibility of becoming irrelevant again. We are supposed to see these mean girls as irredeemable bullies, yet I contend that there is more we should consider about their characters; specifically, Selah and Amy lack emotional safety and therefore use meanness and opacity as coping strategies to ensure their social status.

Feared by others and represented as going against cultural norms and their friends, Selah in *Selah and the Spades* and Amy in *Cuties* encourage us to consider how Black girls are not allowed to speak about their emotional well-being or show their insecurities except through meanness in popular culture. Their desire to be wanted, particularly at the loss of their fathers and the biting criticism of their mothers, manifests as their need to control others. Placing these beliefs on Black girls, rather than the systems and people that demonize them, recasts misogynoir as personal failing and narcissism. While both characters find self-acceptance at the conclusion of the films, the portrayal of Black girls' opacity (which obscures their feelings of fear and insecurity) as meanness reinforces cultural attitudes that adultify them and justify the poor treatment they receive from their parents and others in their lives. These girls internalize how others identify their usefulness or dispensability rather than on their feelings and desires. They create their own sense of usefulness, which for Selah and Amy breeds manipulative "mean girl" behaviors in their clamor to remain in the spotlight.

Selah's Sanctuary and Prison

The Haldwell School is an elite private boarding school, just south of Philadelphia, Pennsylvania. The school allows day students and boarding students to grace its halls, and its administrators expect excellence at every turn. As Principal Banton (Jesse Williams) admonishes in an announcement to the students after they had a party after curfew, "You're the best of the best. We have an expectation that you are going to bring that out in each other and not waste yourselves. Maybe not waste all of your talent, maybe not squander all of your potential on childish games. Do better."[4] Haldwell School students are elite and therefore expected to be "better" than children, better than who they are. As the leader of one of the school factions, Selah internalizes this pressure to be excellent from the administrators as well as her mother who regularly communicates her displeasure about Selah's school performance and behavior. Selah feels intense anxiety about her ability to be perfect, in all ways. As captain of the Spirit Squad (cheerleaders) and leader of the Spades—a group known for their steady supply of "booze, pills, powders, fun" to the student body—she presents herself as a boarding school kingpin.[5]

Shown sitting on a rattan peacock chair (also called "Manila chair") reminiscent of photographer Bill Staipp's iconic 1967 image of Black Panther Party leader Huey P. Newton, Selah exudes confidence and unwavering determination to keep her and the Spades at the center of Haldwell's social scene.[6] Selah always looks cool and calculated, able to keep other members and classmates in line through manipulation, intimidation, and violence. While other factions generally relinquish decision-making power to the Spades, a seemingly calculated strategy to keep their supply of booze and drugs uninterrupted, the greatest antagonism Selah faces is a theater group called the Bobbys led by a white girl, Bobby, who is constantly threatening Selah's status. The structure of this antagonist relationship, as well as the fact that the Spades are almost entirely a Black faction while the Bobbys are a white one, coincides with Selah's perch upon the peacock chair; Black students, especially in elite white spaces, are regularly treated as if they don't belong or are disrespected because of white students' ambitions and fears.[7] Therefore, Selah's allegiance to perfection for herself and those around her, parroted in a comment made several times in the film—"We don't make mistakes"—echoes the cultural lessons that many

Black people get about operating in white spaces—we must be "twice as good."

While there is no direct commentary on race throughout the film, Selah's mother's insistence that she be excellent echoes this sentiment. During a phone call, Selah's mother Maybelle asks about her daughter's recent calculus test. Even though Selah "got a 93," her mother asks, "What happened to the other 7 points?"[8] Selah explains that her schedule has impacted her grade, but Maybelle says, "The older you get, the more like your father you sound. Always with the excuses."[9] This statement not only aligns Selah's less-than-perfect academic performance with moral failing, but it also frames that failing as a lesser quality from Selah's father, who is no longer around. It is not clear whether Selah's father was a man like those who fathered "hip-hop's daughters," who actively used his daughter to cover for his mistakes and excused his misogynist behavior as the simple yet expected failings of a man. However, the use of his excuses as fodder in Selah and Maybelle's conversations communicates that Selah feels the need to protect him from her mother's obvious disdain. His absence, Maybelle's comments about him, and Selah's protection of him echoes other Black fathers in popular films and the idea that Black men loom large in the disagreements between Black girls and Black women; and yet, this exchange as well as others between mother and daughter in the film communicate Selah's feelings of insecurity and belittlement because of her mother. While her mother surely loves her, the tone and communication patterns indicate a strained and tense relationship wherein Selah associates shame and stress with their relationship. Selah always releases a deep sigh when they talk, she approaches her mother timidly, and there are never affectionate gestures or looks shared between them. Whereas she feels powerless and cowers under her mother's antagonisms, Selah seems to replicate these interactions with the students at Haldwell. She is the powerful one there and does whatever necessary to keep that position intact.

Selah's relationship with her mother provides little reassurance that Selah can be herself and be accepted anywhere. At Haldwell, this means Selah's confidence is shakily built to hide her feelings of inadequacy. She is unable to ever make mistakes or show vulnerability to anyone, and she requires the same of Spades members. The film narrator indicates that Selah's struggle at Haldwell is about "what she must do in order to ensure her legacy, seeing as it's the spring semester of her senior year and she has no one to pass her power down to."[10] Although the Spades have been reigning for years, the Bobbys' leader indicates that she is "willing to take over" if Selah cannot secure the future of the Spades' power. Therefore, Selah's introduction of a new second-in-command to the Spades, a sophomore named Paloma, is necessary to cement its reign. But this very inclusion is what seems to make Selah unravel.

Although she and Maxxie—her steady lieutenant who carries out violent attacks and maintains the ledger for their products and services—have been leading the Spades together for years and covering up various mistakes she has made, Selah sees relationships of any kind as distractions. As she encourages Paloma to get more involved, and increasingly violent to ensure her place in the Spades leadership, Selah also feels threatened by the once quiet and unseen photographer Paloma. While Selah sees her manipulative protection and encouragement of Paloma as necessary to create the proper next leader, Paloma's ability to see Selah's vulnerabilities and challenge her authority makes Selah question her allegiances. Their relationship, as well as Maxxie's interest in a new girl which makes him less reliable and therefore less trustworthy in Selah's and Paloma's eyes, fuels much of the film's action. But the emotional pulse of the film follows Selah's every move.

More than the Bobbys' or even Paloma's ambitions, Selah is constantly threatened by her own perceptions of herself. She practices smiling and using a calm tone in the mirror.[11] She uses a combination of intimidation, violence, and secrets to keep others at arms' length. She is fearful of the loss of her hypervisibility and control, forcing her to prove her usefulness and others' dispensability even when it harms her. Under her tutelage, Paloma becomes the budding leader and organizer she needs to be in order to push the Spades forward, but Selah sees her growth as a threat rather than a connection she can make between her and another Black girl.

Selah's character seems to be a manifestation of other Black girls I've discussed throughout; she is confronted by the idea of being fast, she must redeem her father's mistakes through her own attempts at perfection, and she feels that her only usefulness is displayed in being a manipulative leader who internalizes hypervisibility as control. Her monologue early in the film during Spirit Squad practice, where she is first introduced to Paloma's photographic eye, elucidates this fact:

> Hey! They make the new kids take our photos cause they don't take us seriously. That's a mistake the whole world makes. They never take the girls seriously. So it's like this. . . . When you're seventeen and you're a girl, you got the whole world telling you what to do with your body. Your mom tells you change your dress, it's too fast, too short, too shiny. The school tells you cover your shoulders, cover your legs, because they can't tell boys to keep it in their pants! And boys [chuckles] they're the worst. They tell you they'll only like you if you look impossible. So you got all these people telling you how to wear your skin, making you feel like whatever you want is the wrong, slutty thing. And then you've got Spirit Squad. You know who decides our uniforms? We do. You know who choreographs our routines? We do. We tell you how short our skirts will be, how high and tight our tucks will reign, how spread out we make our eagles. I mean, if you got a problem with it, well, honestly that's . . . that's your problem. Because we do it for ourselves, for our control over our bodies. Cuz when you're seventeen [scoffs], you've got to grab onto that control wherever you can and hold tight for dear life, cuz they always try to take it from you don't they? They always try and break you down when you're seventeen.[12]

Although Selah is not southern, this monologue bespeaks much of the emotional weight of "fast girl" ideology that I discuss in chapter 1 and the hypervisibility Black girls face in chapter 3. Selah bemoans the expectations that parents, school administrators, and potential suitors have of girls at the age of seventeen. Crushed under hypervisibility for being young and female (and Black), girls like Selah intensely feel the weight of "all these people telling you how to wear your skin, making you feel like whatever you want is the wrong, slutty thing." To Selah and others, pursuing your own desires with your own body is considered "wrong, slutty," and yet she finds autonomy in leading Spirit Squad because they "do it for [them]selves, for [their] control over [their] bodies." Selah's empowered statement however closes with the knowledge that her control is temporary and always under threat: "Cuz when you're seventeen you've got to grab onto that control wherever you can and hold tight for dear life, cuz they always try to take it from you don't they? They always try and break you down." Selah's statement aligns control of her body with doing something for herself, while others demonize her self-autonomy as "wrong, slutty" and threaten to "try and break [her] down" when she doesn't acquiesce to their desires and expectations.

Situated alongside her interactions with her mother, and her own self-proclaimed asexuality because she's "not interested in the thing itself . . . [she sees] girls crying in the bathroom and like why bother," Selah believes relationships only communicate expectations and curtail one's autonomy.[13] She is not interested in romantic relationships or even friendships because of her own beliefs about how those connections require that she do what someone else wants. This belief permeates all her interactions—even those with Maxxie and Paloma, because ultimately, she sees them as her soldiers rather than her friends in a Haldwell war for importance—and results from her internalizing hypervisibility and intimidation as power; she's willing to do what is necessary to protect herself from them even as they impart trust and love to her.

While Selah's approach positions her as the most powerful and therefore untouchable of all Haldwell students, her anxiety and tears throughout the film communicate her pain and lack of emotional safety. In front of others, she is all-powerful; but in her room or alone with Paloma, her façade fails her. Selah is deeply anxious about her ability to control her own life and her body. She's fearful of allowing others too close to her vulnerabilities because they might, like her mother, seek only to control her. She's insecure about her abilities to lead and therefore uses the threat of violence and manipulative rhetoric to stave off others like the Bobbys and Paloma from taking over. While I do not excuse behavior that endangers her safety and others' lives, Selah's behavior is indicative of a Black girl child who feels there is no other way to maintain control of the things she holds dear.

In her attempts to be the queen Spade, Selah hurts herself and others. While her mother may love her, her constant attempts to choose for Selah rather than allowing Selah to communicate her fears and choose for herself means the spaces where Selah should feel the safest are not safe at all. This relationship, and the absence of her father, bleed onto every other relationship Selah has; it makes her unable to communicate without manipulation or trust others and their intentions. Her meanness then enfolds her feelings of instability and insecurity, trapping her in a cycle of fear and lashing out at those closest to her to protect herself. Selah is then presented as a heartless mercenary rather than a Black girl in need of love and support—a typical trick of misogynoir.

Amy's Anger

Unlike Selah, who is initially presented as a powerful leader of other children at school, Amy in *Cuties* (2020) is first presented as a quiet, obedient Muslim Senegalese girl who only wishes to please her mother. Having relocated to a working-class immigrant neighborhood in France with her mother and two younger brothers, Amy believes her duty as a daughter is to help her mother run the household, running errands, caring for herself and her siblings, and helping to clean the house while her mother is busy. Amy (Fathia

Youssef) begins to stray from her dutiful life when she overhears her mother weeping. Having found out that her husband has taken another wife while away in Senegal, Amy's mother is devastated and seems to withdraw from taking care of her children to cope with her own pain. Forced to call and tell others through feigned happiness about her husband's new nuptials by an older woman in the community only referred to as "Auntie," Amy's mother struggles to make sense of her life while her husband takes care of another. Amy cries too and begins to seek another outlet for her devotion; she despises the pain that her mother experiences and the performance she is required to put on to carry out her "duty" and "be a real woman" as Auntie chides.[14]

Amy begins imagining herself differently after noticing another girl her age in the apartment building laundry room who dances wildly and uses an iron to straight her hair. Seeing the life that lies before her if she follows her mother and Auntie's path—devotion to family and husband even when they cause you pain—Amy sees this girl as another way of being, a vision of glamorous freedom that she can grasp onto as her anger at her father's choices and her mother's performances builds. In a red floral crop top and faux leather pants, midriff bare, the girl represents a life free of duty and servitude where she dictates her joy and does not care what others think. As Amy spends more time around the girl and her friends, she realizes they have their own set of rules that are also based on others' expectations and beliefs. The film follows her struggle to make sense of the expectations (and disappointments) within her Muslim family's life as well as those that govern the seemingly glamorous life non-Muslim girls her age live.

Amy's story is also one of developmental change; the film shows her being instructed in the ways of being a woman such as covering her hair and body around men, praying as a form of piety, and caring for the household as a woman's duty. She also starts menstruating, which seems to even more staunchly push her to find what womanhood looks like for her. As she begins bleeding monthly and growing breasts, Amy starts to see herself differently and notice the ways that women and girls are sexualized through social media and music. After her new friends make fun of her hair, clothes, and flat butt and chest, Amy begins to see the women in her life differently too, deciding that she wants to have a butt like other women in her mother's prayer group. She creates her own social media page and practices kissy faces, then begins to experience the exhilaration of social media likes and the power she feels when others notice and "reward" her for sexualizing herself.

Over the course of the film, we witness Amy begin to steal, lie, and become violent toward others to maintain her social blossoming. When the girl in the crop top, Angelica, finally notices her, Amy becomes a devotee of Angelica's outfits and temperament. Whereas the other girls in the group, Yasmine, Jess, and Coumba, continue to be suspicious of and mean toward her, Angelica spends time with her and discusses her own issues with her family. This endears Amy even more, turning her quiet awe into violent devotion. Amy would do anything to please Angelica and morphs herself more and more to fit Angelica's image. Once Yasmine betrays Angelica's trust, Amy dutifully steps up to take her spot in the group. Through deep study and mimicry, Amy copies their dance routine and adds her own moves taken from sexually suggestive music videos she finds online. Teaching them these moves and showing her own flair for booty popping, Amy becomes a central figure of the group, a righthand to Angelica's vision of winning a local dance competition. Like Selah, her position with her friends however is threatened by her own choices, and she begins to lash out at others to maintain the freedom and importance she thinks she has.

Amy's relevance to the group hinges on her ability to dance and present herself as they do. While critics have focused on the sexualization of girls through dance and social media—the world that *Cuties* builds to let us see through the eyes of young girls like Amy— Amy's transition from quiet and obedient to angry and violent is one that we should pay specific attention to.[15] Her transition—from "homeless" clothes to tight-fitting ones, from frizzy hair pulled back into a puff to large voluminous curls that halo frame her face, from bare face to glittery eyeshadow and pink lip gloss—is easily marked visually because of the stark changes to clothes, face, and hair that occur. However, Amy's temperament and response to other forces in her life bespeak a larger issue around how Black girls are taught (or not) to cope with the things that happen to them. When Amy catches her mother crying after sharing the news of her father's betrayal, Amy hears her mother smacking herself to control the emotional weight she feels.[16] Not only does this teach Amy how women she is supposed to mimic handle their "duty," but it also shows Amy that her emotions are only those allowed in the solitude of her own space and, even then, should be regulated with self-inflicted violence. While Amy does not hurt herself physically, her choices throughout the film harm her self-esteem and budding understanding of her changing body; these harms further rupture the fragile emotional safety net she already has at home.

When she first encounters Jess, Coumba, and Yasmine, they bully her.[17] They talk negatively about her clothes, body, and hair. They say she looks worse than a homeless person and call her homeless rather than her name. They take her bookbag and throw her papers and books on the ground. They are mean. While Yasmine leaves the group as Amy is included, Jess and Coumba regularly remind her that she is not truly one of them. When they are mean to her or ignore her, Angelica—the leader and the one that is closest to Amy—says nothing. Already desperate for the approval of others, a consequence of her community's insistence that girls' duties are to please their mothers, Amy clings emotionally and physically to whatever closeness she feels with Angelica. But again and again, Angelica abandons her by saying nothing or walking away. As her desperation grows, so does her violent outbursts. After witnessing Angelica use anger to justify hitting her former friend Yasmine, Amy understands that violent displays of anger are justified responses for girls like her and that her own violent actions will endear Angelica; in turn, she gets more and more physically and emotionally violent toward others.[18]

After befriending Angelica, Amy ignores her brother; she stabs a boy in class with a pen; she pushes Yasmine into a waterway, not knowing that she cannot swim.[19] Amy becomes a mean girl. Whereas her mother hides her emotional state and avoids her motherly duties when in distress, teaching Amy to be despondent when disappointed, Amy learns from Angelica that being forceful is another way to respond. She also learns that whatever violent act she takes up is justified because she is angry or sad or distrustful. This emotional chasm between her mother's inaction and Angelica's violent action ultimately overwhelms Amy. As an eleven-year-old Black girl, Amy has still not figured out how to voice her own opinions. Her encounters with the other girls only seem to reinforce the quiet, invisible experience she has at home. When she is no longer sidekick or dutiful daughter, Amy is attacked and belittled. Whereas Selah has several opportunities to speak throughout *Selah and the Spades*, Amy rarely speaks about her own feelings or perceptions of her experiences. When she does speak, it is in reference to her father or in desperate response to others.

Amy in many ways represents Black girls who are navigating pressure from all sides with little opportunity to communicate their own concerns; over the course of years in her family and in friendships with other girls, Amy learns that her value is in how she performs for others. Using her body as labor for the home or as desirable object for social media likes, Amy learns that her usefulness is really about others' valuation of her and that that valuation is based on how they can use her.[20] Both her relationship with her mother and with Angelica bear this conclusion. Neither are interested in Amy's desires, needs, or fears outside of what they might need from her. While Amy pushes the dance crew to become more and more provocative in search of what it means to be "real women," they abandon her.[21]

When Amy gets home, her mother invites their mosque's Imam to pray for her; while there is no conversation about Amy's willingness to be touched or prayed over by him, he tells the mother, "I know what you're going through with your husband is very difficult, but God has never imposed on women more than they could bear. If your burden is too heavy, you have the right to leave this marriage. But know this: there is no devil or spirit here," as he gestures toward Amy.[22] In both cases, Amy is being evaluated based on others' needs for her and her refusal to do as she is told. Her provocativeness goes too far for the other girls, while her unwillingness to be a dutiful daughter in the way her mother wants is evaluated for evil spirits. Amy's meanness then is an outgrowth of her lack of outlet; she has no one to communicate with and no one with whom she feels there is no expectation of devotion or labor from her. The one person that she might feel close to and from whom she can expect gifts and praise, her father, has seemingly abandoned her as well.

Where Are Black Girls Safe?

Both Selah and Amy are fueled by fear and use violence to barricade their vulnerabilities from others. They have no outlet for the questions they have, no person with whom communication is unguarded. They both struggle to find a balance between their mothers' chastisement and the lack of support from their friends. They both seek safety from men in their lives who are not present, but they also use the lack of validation of their feelings and concerns to justify their violent behavior toward others. They are unwilling to take responsibility for their actions, both because they haven't been taught to do so and because they believe they carry responsibility for so many other things. Indeed, neither of them really have friends, and their daily lives are structured by what they provide for others or whether they are meeting others' expectations. Written by Black women, these stories speak to their own experiences as well as demonstrate a larger issue around emotional safety for Black girls.

As exemplified by Selah's inability to connect with her mother and Paloma, and Amy's shouldering of familial expectations regardless of the disappointment and fear she feels, the space for Black girls' emotional safety is elusive. They learn in institutional settings and at home that they cannot trust anyone with their true feelings. They learn from friends and family that their emotional state is trumped by the labor others need them to do; tears and fear are not ways that Black girls can communicate and be heard. For both Selah and Amy, this lack of emotional safety breeds narcissism and manipulation. They believe for others to care about them, they must prove their utility or force codependency from others who are more assured and confident than they feel.

As both well-regarded and controversial films, *Selah and the Spades* and *Cuties* show the precarious nature of Black girls' worlds. Black girls are unsafe and regularly feel like they must fight to create opportunities to be seen. Their parents as well as friends and school administrators ignore the problematic relationships they have with them, and instead, require them to fend for themselves. More pointedly, the so-called outrage about the sexualization of girls that conversative political leaders crafted when *Cuties* was released on Netflix in 2020 further instantiates the lack of concern for actual girls; the reality of girls like Amy and Selah participating and crafting their own narratives around sexuality (which is the framing of *Cuties*) is less important than the idea that adults have about them or how these films allow us to see the harm that we are all complicit in when we force girls into preconceived notions about who they are.

Thus far, I have considered instances of mostly physical harm that Black girls experience in fantastical situations. The adults in their lives as well as their friends are ill-equipped to truly see them and instead perpetuate misogynoir. I conclude here considering representations of Black girls' emotional safety in more realistic settings. Whether they are in situations we recognize or fantastical locales, recent representations of Black girls in critically acclaimed films reward others for disrespecting and harming them. Black girls in turn are taught that their only means to emotional and physical safety, as well as futures where they are active participants, is by proving their utility (forcing others to not dispose of them when they would like) or crafting narratives of their own making through manipulation and violence. These examples lead us to the death-dealing experiences Black girls have at every level of US society as well as the ideological beliefs that make Black girls hypervisible yet disposable—multiple layers of failure that harm and eventually kill Black girls. Moving forward, I map possible pathways to healing that are available for Black girls and the communities where they live. I believe through deep emotional work that challenges our notions of individuality, control, and wellness, we can embark on new pathways for Black girls in real life and in popular culture.

EPILOGUE

Finding Healing in Failure

> To imagine a version of liberation that is capacious enough to include those of us who are farthest from the hegemonic center entails a rethinking of our relations to each other, which in turn entails a rethinking of power.
> —Habiba Ibrahim, *Black Age*

> When I speak of love, I speak of community and a type of nurturing environment that allows my writer self and my Black girl self to live uninhibited.... And I like my love sugarcaned, honey-dipped, and fluorescent, a neon advertisement kind of love, billboard-style love and big enough to read when you are way down the highway and told to you in many tongues.
> —DaMaris B. Hill, *Breath Better Spent*

Black Girls and How We Fail Them is an outgrowth of anger. Informed by my own frustration with the ways I and other girls of color have been treated by those who are supposed to love and care for us as well as Audre Lorde's 1981 NWSA keynote address on the "uses of anger," this book takes seriously our individual and collective complicity in Black girls' trauma.[1] Making my anger productive, as Lorde encourages, I map the discourses that frame how collective beliefs about Black girls and their experiences are manufactured within widely distributed, easily streamable, and, at times, controversial films of the past decade. I consider how media platforms like Netflix,

Amazon Prime, Disney+, and others inform US and diasporic engagements with Black girls in leading roles, locating cinematic representations that promote hatred toward Black girls for the evolution of others. I consider where Black girls are missing from our critical discussions about representation, care, and blackness, and how we have been complicit in depicting Black girls as unwanted and disposable.

Over the past five years, I have written several articles and a book about the relationship between Black women cultural producers and Black girlhood. I specifically argued that Black girls can interpret and use Black women's cultural production, especially that which utilizes aspects of Black cultural knowledge to craft material and visual objects, for their benefit. Contemporary narratives surrounding the murders of Renisha McBride, Breonna Taylor, and most recently Ma'Khia Bryant, however, have made me consider how we discuss Black girls within popular discourses.[2] I wondered what images and dialogues encouraged people to see Black girls as justifiable victims of state-sanctioned and extrajudicial violence. The undercurrents that guided me throughout this book located Black girls within the discourse of other people that characterized them as fast, yet dispensable tools. I considered how Black girls' experiences were explained, how their bodies were read, and how their emotions were contextualized as part of the narrative plot for critically acclaimed films. I challenged us to see how others interacted with and discussed Black girl characters as well as how Black girls responded to their treatment. Through questioning how the popular films, public conversations and podcasts, and political debates we engage with encourage misogynoir toward Black girls—even as we have become vigilant about the ways Black women are treated and represented—I pushed us to consider how popular culture informs the stories we tell about Black girls, about their bodies, and about the terrible things that happen to them.

I found that whether discussing fictional or real Black girls, their US pop culture representations depend on our collective dismissal of their pain. We valorize violence particularly for those who "deserve" it, and, within pop culture, Black girls always deserve it. We value them as physical and discursive pillars to hold up others as they progress toward actualization. We honor them for resiliency and survival with no redress for the harm they experience in the process. We acknowledge the lack of resources we grant to them as they are pushed out, disrespected, and violated by systems of white supremacy and sexism, but do little to address the people that reify these ideas. My hopes in writing *Black Girls and How We Fail Them* were twofold: that Black girls see themselves anew in the popular culture of the 2010s and 2020s and that we shift our collective commitments to their safety and well-being. Ultimately, to become the community we contend that we are, we must accept that we have failed.

We have failed generations of Black girls by participating in their erasure and surveillance. We have attempted to control everything about their existence supposedly for their safety, and yet Black girls are still unsafe. Our households, our community centers and places of worship, our entertainment spaces, our collective imaginary has made it unsafe for Black girls to be themselves and express when they feel unsafe. We have made them the problems for advocating for themselves, for telling people how they should treat them, and for resisting disrespect and discomfort for the benefit of others. But I believe there is a pathway toward healing ourselves and our community that does not rely on Black girls going missing. Therefore, I beckon to what it means to be Black and a girl in a world that, in the words of Malcolm X, teaches you to despise yourself.[3] I consider how we might approach healing through an understanding of our individual and collective failure and that that acceptance can liberate us from the practices of misogynoir I have discussed throughout this book.

Here, I revisit Audre Lorde's *Cancer Journals* to excavate Black feminist healing theories and practices for Black girls. Lorde's theories about healing specifically speak to Black girls' experiences dealing with the disease of misogynoir, which is embedded not only in the ways they see themselves and their friends but also in how their families, their communities, and the larger society sees them.

Lorde's concept of healing ourselves provides both the theory and practice that Black girls and women must embrace for liberation from misogynoir.

In addition to how Black girls and women have failed themselves by internalizing misogynoir and others' need for them, failure also has implications for others, and rejecting misogynoir can liberate all of us rather than leaving Black girls to fend for themselves. Beyond the healing that Black girls and women must do, others must heal from misogynoir and the work that patriarchy has done on them. I encourage us to find healing through our acknowledgment of failure, by attending to failure as a lack of accountability, and by recognizing that both healing and failure together will help us craft a liberatory future for all.

Healing Ourselves

The experiences of Black girls—the fast-girl rhetoric thrown at Keke, the hypervisibility and surveillance of Malia and Sasha, the savior mentality pushed on Hushpuppy and Melanie, the salvific stance forced on Robin and Meg, the insecurity felt by Selah and Amy—illustrate how Black girls cope with misogynoir in every aspect of how they interact with the world around them. While they are described as fast, mean, aggressive, hostile, and manipulative, they are shown to be caring, adaptive, observant, loving, scared, confused, and anxious. They represent girls across the diaspora who are actively trying to find their place in a world that tells them they do not matter nor are they useful beyond what they can do for others. Misogynoir circumscribes their lives to violent and abusive interactions and mischaracterizations by those observing them and their actions. Yet Black girls continually manifest different ways of being, doing, and interacting that center their beliefs about themselves. The level of violence and abuse with which these girls cope is indicative of a need for healing, both from internalized misogynoir and the trauma incurred by the mistreatment Black girls have faced.

The 2022 critically acclaimed film *The Woman King*, directed by

Gina Prince-Blythewood, attends to the aftermath of trauma for Black girls and women. Though I am not analyzing the film in its entirety, I do wish to name the deep trauma experienced by Nawi, the headstrong daughter who defies her father's desire to marry her off and who becomes an Agojie warrior. In several moments throughout the film, Nawi is told she is arrogant and that her decisions to support her fellow sister-warriors or follow her own intuition about people and events will get her and others killed. After a prank on the Agojie generals, Nawi is punished and told that her easy life will not get her anywhere in the group. Although she should not talk, she cries repeatedly: "I have not had an easy life!"[4] This statement and the belief that she is arrogant, rather than scared and working to build trust in her own instincts, likens her to the eight other girls in this book. Nawi has had to trust only herself, as an adopted child who has worked hard to stymie fear. Her so-called arrogance manifests much like Keke's and Selah's self-assuredness, Robin's and Amy's defiance, Hushpuppy's refusal of social customs, and Robin's and Melanie's decisions to create futures for others. Constantly watched and judged like Malia and Sasha, Nawi fortifies herself even in a community of Black women. They rail against her protection of others and her belief in herself, but it is ultimately her beliefs and confidence that secure victory for everyone in future battles. Nawi and these other examples therefore illustrate a need for us to not only better understand Black girls' strategies for emotional fortification, but to also unlearn misogynoir that encourages us to read Black girls as arrogant and defiant despite their actual feelings. Whether written and directed by Black women or someone else, the trope of Black girls as disposable reoccurs. Hence, the work we need to do for Black girls is for all of us.

I found, as did feminist author bell hooks in her own book about Black women's healing, *Sisters of the Yam*, that Audre Lorde provides necessary guidance for our survival. hooks explains,

> Black female self-recovery, like all black self-recovery, is an expression of a liberatory political practice. Living as we do

in a white-supremacist capitalist patriarchal context that can best exploit us when we lack a firm grounding in self and identity (knowledge of who we are and where we have come from), choosing "wellness" is an act of political resistance. Before many of us can effectively sustain engagement in organized resistance struggle, in black liberation movement, we need to undergo a process of self-recovery that can heal individualized wounds that may prevent us from functioning fully.[5]

Therefore, in search of "black self-recovery" for Black girls and women that heal "individual wounds," we follow Lorde's theories about healing specifically to speak to Black girls' experiences dealing with the disease of misogynoir. Black girls can heal the individual wounds created by their self-perception as well as by how others, like their friends, their families, their communities, and the larger society, see them.

HEALING WITH LORDE

Although Audre Lorde is forty-four at the time of her mastectomy in *The Cancer Journals*, she recounts thinking about Dahomey Amazons on several occasions—girls aged fifteen who she considers warriors alongside her own journey because of the myth that they have a right breast removed to become better archers. While there is little support for this myth in scholarship about these African women warriors, Lorde thinks often about the girls' ability to let go of parts of themselves to be better warriors. Lorde, in many ways, considers herself a warrior like them, fighting for her life against cancer and the "grey mush" of her brain caused by anesthesia.[6] Beyond obvious parallels among Lorde, the fictional idea of girl warriors in her journals, and the group of girls and women displayed in Gina Prince-Blythewood's *The Woman King*, Lorde describes her loss akin to these girls and presents healing as a painful process that we should want to be reminded of, even when it requires loss. Through Lorde's journey I wonder what healing really looks like for Black girls and women scarred by misogynoir and how our own internalized beliefs about ourselves render us invisible to ourselves.

The girls I describe throughout this book are forced to be useful and are made hypervisible through their utility. By family members, community leaders, friends, school administrators, church members, or social media users, Keke, Malia, Sasha, Hushpuppy, Melanie, Robin, Meg, Selah, and Amy are all seen—not because of their own beauty, quirkiness, or aptitude, but because they have become useful to someone else's narrative about them or to someone else's self-evolution. They are made visible because others overdetermine their purpose, arguing that whatever they want or desire for themselves is less useful than the desires of others. Black girls, especially those that are dark-skinned, thick-bodied, or loud-mouthed, have had to prove their utility through self-denial, moving them emotionally and physically further away from themselves and their perceptions of themselves and toward others' characterizations.

A pivotal point in *The Cancer Journals* is when Audre Lorde describes a nurse's chastisement of her for not wearing a silicone breast prosthesis during her postsurgery checkup and therefore ruining the morale of others in the doctor's office. Lorde rails against the idea that her perception of her body should be less important to her than others' perceptions of it. She says: "I am personally affronted by the message that I am only acceptable if I look 'right' or 'normal,' where those norms have nothing to do with my own perceptions of who I am. Where ... a woman's perception of her own body and the strengths that come from that perception are discouraged, trivialized, and ignored."[7] Instead, she offers, "In order to keep me available to myself, and able to concentrate my energies upon those challenges of those worlds through which I move, I must consider what my body means to me. I must also separate those external demands about how I look and feel to others, from what I really want for my own body, and how I feel to my selves."[8] These two statements are of the utmost importance for us, as Black girls and women attempting to heal from and disrupt misogynoir, because we are constantly inundated with the ideas of rightness as described by others. Even as

Black people have historically crafted their own measures of beauty and character in concert with and in opposition to white supremacy, there are rules about so-called Black authenticity that we have also been subject to and are used against us when we do not claim them as our own. Lorde offers us not only a pathway to rejection of those externally determined ideas of ourselves but also a buoy in the sea of perceptions we are awash in every day.

Lorde asks herself, and models that we should ask ourselves: How do I feel about my body? How do I feel about myself? Any information or ideas that are beyond that are not our concern, and we should adamantly deny them entry in our emotional well-being. These questions and our answers to them are pivotal to our healing. Whether the daughters of the most important Black man in America (Malia and Sasha), the last Black girl alive in the apocalypse (Melanie), or the only Black girl who can enfold the universe (Meg), we can only heal when we prioritize our own physical and emotional well-being. But that is the opposite of what we are taught to do, because how will others use us if we do not care about their desires? If we are not subject to others' rules of utility and only bounded by our own limitations, how might the world be different for Black girls and women like us? How might *we* be different if our only struggle is knowing how we feel about ourselves and our bodies? Healing ourselves from the lies of misogynoir, then, is not a self-aggrandizing attempt for power over others but instead is a necessary step toward the lives we say we want.

HURTING TO HEAL: BLACK GIRL SELF-RECOVERY

When Lorde says "in order to keep me available to myself," she presents both the possibility for healing and the dangers of embracing external expectations and perceptions. To be available to oneself, Lorde argues that you must consider what your body means to you. The inverse however is that being made visible to yourself through others' makes you unavailable to yourself. Throughout each film, we see Black girls facing this dilemma over and over. When Selah stands in the mirror practicing how she looks to others as she smiles and talks, she distances herself from her body. When Melanie does not eat in favor of being caged by others so that she can please them, she distances herself from her needs. When Amy feels more validation from social media likes and others' attention, she creates a chasm between her emotional self and her physical one. To be available to yourself is to be structured and affirmed by your own needs and desires, focusing your utility and purpose on your innermost perceptions. The further we get from our bodies, the less available we are to understand what we need.

Robin's character in *Project Power* bears out this conclusion. While she becomes available to others throughout the film, there is constant friction between what she believes is right and good and what others expect or want from her. By becoming more in tune with her power, she frees another Black girl from bondage, while doing what she needs *and* helping her mother. Her power, unlike that which is presented in the film, is really in her ability to keep herself available to herself. Meg in *A Wrinkle in Time* similarly learns that she can help her father and brother once she has come to terms with her perceptions of herself. Even when failed by others—irrespective of whether that results in Black girls rebuking others, characterized by Amy going against her family's wishes in search of herself or by Keke communicating to Micah the appropriate way to talk to and interact with her—Black girls keeping themselves available to their own needs will always bear positive experiences. Going against her family ultimately gave Amy the information she needed to pull away from the so-called friends that bullied her and find a space for herself that did not have to conform to her mother's pain or Auntie's lived experiences. Hushpuppy too becomes "King of the Bathtub" by doing what she thinks is necessary for her own survival. These choices may hurt others initially and may irreparably change Black girls' relationships with everyone else, but these changes will produce a world where others are invited to heal, too. As Lorde puts it, "Self scrutiny and an evaluation of our lives, while painful, can be rewarding and strengthening journeys toward a deeper self. For as we open ourselves more and more to the genuine conditions of our lives, women becomes less and less willing to tolerate those conditions unaltered, or to passively accept external and destructive controls over our lives and our identities."[9] Lorde reminds us that the process of healing is painful and that taking seriously our own needs and desires will cause others pain too because we become less malleable and accepting of the poor treatment we receive from them and ourselves.

Misogynoir, as an extension of white supremacy, requires soldiers to actualize its ideological warfare; said differently, the distinct hatred toward Black girls that we see throughout popular culture and the lived experiences of girls requires complicit individuals to perform hate. Institutional and cultural hatred requires that people believe and act upon their beliefs that Black girls are fast, mean, aggressive, and therefore unworthy of protection, love, or insight unless in service to someone else. People must believe that Black girls are commonsense victims of sexual, physical, and emotional violence and that other girls are not, so we should rally on the latter's behalf. People must believe that life requires control and intimidation to survive. Those people include Black girls and Black women, too—yes, you and me. We believe and perform misogynoir because we believe that our survival is dependent on someone else's utility for our benefit. As I like to say to my friends, we are all trash and are the villains in someone else's story, no matter how good we think we are.

And yet again, Lorde has insight to help us unlearn this. She says, "I carry tattooed upon my heart a list of names of women who did not survive, and there is always a space left for one more, my own. That is to remind me that even survival is only part of the task. The other part is teaching. I had been in training for a long time."[10] We, as Lorde explains, have been trained to only think of survival and to think that our survival requires the death of others. However, our names are always waiting to be added to the list of those who did not survive. We cannot only survive; we must teach ourselves how to live differently, how to expand our lives beyond what misogynoir has taught us. I ask you, as I ask myself, when will we tire of the death-dealing beliefs of misogynoir. It will not save us from the list of those who are no longer here and able to fight, nor will it keep us alive long enough to find other ways of being. Misogynoir will continue to kill us. We must start now.

Failure

Popular representations of Black girls rely on misogynoir to accept violence toward Black girls as realistic and therefore commonsense. We can counteract this by examining and understanding the ways Black girls have been characterized in popular media and by working to heal the nefarious impacts of misogynoir as it presents Black girls as fast, mean, aggressive, manipulative, and ultimately disposable unless they are in service of others. But how do we move from being villains in others' stories toward healing?

Here, I want to revisit an underlying idea of this book that I broach in the "Hip-Hop's Daughters" chapter more explicitly about Black men and others who ultimately use Black girls as their evolutionary Stairmaster. It is an easy impulse to consider others who have failed Black girls—we can identify them when they are external to us, but my hope in this book is not only to identify Black men or boys, but Black women and girls, Black community spaces like churches and mosques, Black entertainers and creatives—all of us have failed. We have left Black girls to fend for themselves. Beyond the healing that Black girls and women must do, I argue others must also heal from misogynoir and the work that patriarchy has done on us. I believe that we must embrace healing as failure, because healing is an imperfect process at which we will fail many times, and hurt each other, as we figure out how to be and do better for ourselves and those we love. Failure then means we must lead with vulnerability and embrace the fear of imperfection. The ugliness of our world cannot be fixed with editing software and social media filters, nor the overrepresentation of Black girls as lead characters (especially in violent stories). Healing will not come without failure, honesty, and vulnerability. So let me start first.

Despite the overrepresentation of Black fatherlessness in contemporary media, I grew up with a father. He was absent for the most part, due to his own prioritizing of money and sex with women who weren't his wife, but I have a father. My dad embraced fancy clothes, women, alcohol, and other things to cure his insatiable desire to matter in a white supremacist capitalist society that told him, as a Black man, he did not matter without those markers of success. He and my mother, though high school sweethearts, were incompatible in their values when it came to parenting. Whereas my father, and many men of his generation, believed that childrearing was a responsibility of women, my mother considered parenting a choice that both individuals in a partnership make. That choice (whether planned or not) ultimately takes all priority over other choices. My father disagreed.

Their disagreements were sometimes violent, particularly when my father was unhappy, and usually resulted in my older sister and I witnessing deeply problematic interactions. At times, my father's violent tendencies were also used against us when we said or did anything he did not like. I recall at one point him hitting me in the head with our landline phone because I repeated something rude—but true—he had said about the person on the phone. He was volatile, and we learned very early to live different lives when he was home compared to when he was not. We would go from boisterous performances with vocals and full choreography of Mariah Carey, Whitney Houston, and the Spice Girls for our mother in the living room to quietly playing games or reading books in our room. We learned that we were not safe to be who we were because of my father's violence. We learned too that even when she tried to protect us, my mother could not always anticipate his violent episodes and was struggling to protect herself too.

By the time my baby sister was born, we had all become disillusioned with my father's attitudes; my older sister and I still wanted our father to love us and show us affection, but we knew he couldn't without also being violent or manipulative. When we finally left my father and my mom was trying to raise three girls by herself, I think we all blossomed. Together, my mother, my sisters, and I sought refuge in each other and built a life that binds us tighter than any other relationships I have ever had. We also sought refuge in our community, many of whom justified his actions as "Men will be men" and "What do you do to make him angry?" Family, church, and social community taught us that we should not name the harm we experienced, nor would they intervene on our behalf to challenge him. Even now, I am sure people in that community would think it bad form to expose "family laundry" in a public, scholarly text.

Twenty years later, however, the years of abuse and neglect from my father still make it difficult to feel safe around men or people that justify men's violence. All the women in my family have experienced some form of assault or manipulative behavior from men. All the women in my family have felt unsafe because of the disrespectful or even violent behavior of men in workplaces or in intimate relationships. As I've aged, I've met more and more women of many racial and ethnic groups who have experienced similar if not the same experiences with men, too. I've also learned that our complicity in violence is not only based on fear, but on our own beliefs about what we deserve and why. Statistically, these experiences have gotten worse rather than better, despite organizations and policy decisions; when recessions, layoffs, or breakups occur, we know that the danger to the lives of women and children by the men in their lives skyrockets.

We have failed to make our society a safe place for girls, and this is a failure we share no matter our gender identity or racial background. We have seminars and kickboxing classes; we have lectures, podcasts, and reams of paper; we have agencies and organizations—all dedicated to creating a safer society for all of us, and yet the violence continues. We are not safe, and although we have been raised as I was to still be excellent despite chaotic and violent environments—to prove that our mothers and caregivers could still give us a good life and we could still be successful—we cannot continue to raise any children in an unsafe environment. Whether in Sandy Hook or Uvalde, we teach children that violence is routine and therefore commonsense. We teach children that violence is even necessary for our society to continue, and those we have lost along the way are simply casualties in the war of life. But in addition to the people we've lost, we need to think seriously about what we are losing within ourselves, if we continue to fail.

We do not fail because we do not know where our failure occurs. We fail because we believe failure is the best we can do and therefore choose not to change. Audre Lorde explains this idea in two ways: "For silence and invisibility go hand in hand with powerlessness," and "We reinforce our own isolation and invisibility from each other, as well as the false complacency of a society which would rather face the results of its own insanities. In addition, we withhold that visibility and support from one another which is such an aid to perspective and self-acceptance."[11] Through my analysis of Black women's writing since the 1980s it is evident that Black women have been telling each other and their families about the pain they experience as girls. They have published their stories and been ridiculed or disrespected when they do. Still, we have been talking about our experiences with each other, and in more contemporary times, seeking mental health services and self-help books as well as seminars and sermons to help understand our experiences and how not to recreate them.

However, we as Black women who seek to forgo our silence and be seen apart from the strong or asexual stereotypes are still subject to violence. The rest of our community struggles to explain, name, and uncover traumatic and abusive experiences, and we collectively fail to name and seek consequences for those who harm us. Predators, narcissists, and manipulative people *within our communities* thrive on our inability to call them out and force them to make amends for the harm they have done in the name of love, protection, or God. They manipulate the danger we experience and fear we have due to racism and white supremacy to keep us in silence. But like the women who have spoken out against Robert Kelly, William Cosby, Sean Combs, and other predators among us, we must decide our girls (and boys) matter more than whatever gifts we believe these people offer. Is creativity the cost of Black girl lives? Is "the culture" worth our silence? We must decide *we* matter more and that we deserve better. When we decide to name our pain, call out those among us who have caused harm in whatever ways need to be said, and move ourselves away from isolation, we can change what is happening. When we create and sustain community that is just and therefore loving to the most vulnerable of us, change is possible in and around us. When we decide that our lives individually and collectively matter more than shame or fame, we have the opportunity for cultural change.

Sacrificing Black girls and ourselves to those who harm results not only in the kind of critically acclaimed but deeply problematic films discussed here but also in the creation and propagation of false ideas about who Black girls are in political spaces, on talk shows, and in Black girl-focused organizations I analyze throughout this book. Through surveillance in person and on social media, we contort ourselves and Black girls to fit our abusers' desires. Those ideas do not become muddled as these girls age—as we age, they get coupled with other problematic ideas and dangerous interactions, further ingraining the idea that we are not worthy of protection, that our experiences are not important to understand, that our feelings are not necessary to express or honor. And because we eventually believe these lies about ourselves and our experiences, we become complicit in their circulation; we stay in relationships that are characterized by mistreatment and distrust, we see scared and anxious Black girls as angry and arrogant, and we explain away violence as a typical consequence for doing things others do not like. We justify abuse by refusing to maintain any fidelity to ourselves; we choose others over ourselves and our needs and therefore fail, repeatedly. And our art and conversations reflect our allegiances.

But our previous failures do not have to dictate our futures. We can make the world safe for us by embracing our duty to our inner selves. Our duty to ourselves is the same as our duty to Black girls— we must accept that we have failed to protect ourselves and them. We must face the lies we believe and spread. We must name the ways we have been complicit, including the lies we've told to protect the abusive people among us, the lessons we've ingrained in girls and women in our community to accept disrespect, dishonesty, and violence as typical characteristics of relationships with men and each other, and the silences we keep when we or they are laid to rest for fear of "speaking ill of the dead." We must choose to learn new ways of being for the sake of our communities, our girls, and ourselves. Healing is possible when we claim failure and see it as an opportunity for change.

In the pursuit of survival, we have failed by sacrificing ourselves and our girls to the violence of white supremacy and patriarchy. We've let protection, in the form of value constructed by men, keep us apart and create narratives about who is worthy of protection and who is not. We have been complicit based on faulty logic and false generosity, but we don't have to be. Through therapy, truth, and sisterly community, we can navigate and change the world we experienced for our daughters and sons, but most importantly, for ourselves.

RESOURCES FOR FAILING LESS

Below I provide a short list of resources that I have found useful—these are places to begin confronting our complicity, to begin learning differently, to embrace abundance, sisterhood, honesty, and faith as tools that can buoy us in the process of healing. As I have attempted to map the pain of misogynoir, I include these resources to show us paths to healing from it. When in doubt, seek out a friend. Read a book. Listen to your inner voice. We are not alone, nor are we without options.

Finding Me by Viola Davis

Eloquent Rage by Brittney Cooper

Dressed in Dreams by Tanisha Ford

Walk through Fire by Sheila Johnson

Red Lip Theology by Candice Marie Benbow

Black Girl, Call Home by Jasmine Mans

Breath Better Spent by DaMaris B. Hill

New Black Man by Mark Anthony Neal

All About Love by bell hooks

Homecoming podcast by Thema Bryant

Therapy for Black Girls podcast by Joy Harden Bradford

ACKNOWLEDGMENTS

Sincere gratitude to all who listened to talks about this book or heard me in anguish about what to write and how to write it; thank you so much for hearing me and encouraging me to say what I needed to. To those who have been stumbling blocks on my way to this point, I thank you, too. Without the hurt and pain you caused, I wouldn't be here with all of myself. Special shout-outs to: my sisters, my mom, my boo, my homies Ashleigh Greene Wade, Rayna McKenzie, Tina Beyene, Lauren Whitehurst, Chelsea Privette, Candice Robinson, Therí Pickens; my friend colleagues who supported, checked on, wrote with, cried with, laughed with, and buoyed me—Regina Bradley, Nadia Brown, Regina Hamilton-Townsend, Crystal Felima, Chelsea Frazier, Andrea Adomako, Zachary Levenson, Chanda Prescod-Weinstein, Frances Henderson, Mireille Miller-Young, Daye Rogers, DaMaris Hill, Vanessa Holden, Anastasia Curwood, Derrick White. Thank you to the Black men who spoke with me about their experiences with hip-hop and fatherhood—Chris, Harvey, Frank, Jordan, and Vaughan (Rest in Power, friend). Thank you to the UT Austin community—especially Henry (Adore Nail Lounge), Aaron (Paper Route Bakery), Progress Coffee, Teaspoon, the Harrington Fellowship '22–'23 committee, Charrise Barron, Enjoli Richardson, Ya'Ke Smith, and the incomparable Christen A. Smith. Thank you, Kate Kelly—all our manifesting came true! Thank you, Porsche Lockett—therapy was really the key that unlocked all of this. Thank you, Dawn Durante—you saw the promise of this idea from the beginning, and your support helped bring it to life.

NOTES

INTRODUCTION. FAILURE IS EVERYWHERE
1. Mans, Black Girl, Call Home, 201.
2. Bailey, Misogynoir Transformed.
3. hooks, Black Looks.
4. Noble, Algorithms of Oppression.
5. Butler, "Black Girl Cartography."
6. Perry, Vexy Thing, 23.
7. Halliday, Black Girlhood Studies Collection, 6–8.
8. Ibrahim, Black Age, 47.
9. Lindsey, America, Goddam.
10. Davis, "New Study Shows"; Tounsel, Branding Black Womanhood; Halliday, Buy Black.
11. Halliday, Buy Black.
12. Bryant, "Black Girls Code."
13. Bryant, "Black Girls Code."
14. Halliday and Brown, "Power of Black Girl Magic Anthems."
15. Halliday, Buy Black.

CHAPTER 1. HIP-HOP'S DAUGHTERS
1. Morgan, Chickenheads, 127.
2. Neal, Looking for Leroy, 5.
3. Gonzalez, "Jay-Z's '4:44' Humanizes Him."
4. Morgan, Chickenheads, 74.
5. Morgan, Chickenheads, 75.
6. Shepherd, "Brief Taxonomy of the Fuccboi"; K. Brown, "Definition of 'Fuckboy'"; Brogan, "This Obscene Insult Is Suddenly Everywhere."
7. Perry, Vexy Thing, 21, 27.
8. Perry, Vexy Thing, 27.
9. Perry, Vexy Thing, 18.

10. Gaunt, *Games Black Girls Play*, 118.
11. Rose, *Black Noise*; Pough, *Check It While I Wreck It*; Halliday and Payne, "Twenty-First Century B.I.T.C.H."
12. Vidal, "An Ode to Jay-Z."
13. Benbow, "4:43."
14. Halliday, "Trauma," 39.
15. Benbow, "4:43."
16. Letterman, *My Next Guest*.
17. Oware, "Decent Daddy," 341.
18. Oware, "Decent Daddy," 341.
19. Iton, *In Search of the Black Fantastic*, 153–54.
20. Amber, "No Ordinary Love."
21. Amber, "No Ordinary Love."
22. Amber, "No Ordinary Love."
23. "Kim Porter on Breaking Up," *Essence*.
24. Penn, "Diddy and Daughters Grace the Cover."
25. hampton, "Diddy Is 'Family over Everything.'"
26. hampton, "Diddy Is 'Family over Everything.'"
27. A. Brown, "Sean 'Diddy' Combs Sexual Harassment Suit."
28. Smith, "Rapper T.I. and His Wife."
29. Smith, "T.I. and Tiny."
30. Smith, "T.I. and Tiny."

CHAPTER 2. HYPERVISIBLE BLACK GIRLHOOD

1. Tillet, "Make Revolution Irresistible," 484.
2. Cooper, "A'n't I a Lady?," 50.
3. Noble, *Algorithms of Oppression*, 32–33.
4. Thomas, *Dark Fantastic*, 56.
5. Gaunt, "Youtube, Twerking, & You," 253.
6. Halliday, "Miley, What's Good?," 67.
7. Hartman, *Wayward Lives*, 21.
8. Cox, *Shapeshifters*, 160.
9. Shange, *Progressive Dystopia*.
10. Boffone, *Renegades*.
11. Valdivia, "Living in a Hybrid Material World"; Khoja-Mooljii, *Forging the Ideal Educated Girl*; Projansky, *Spectacular Girls*.
12. Projansky, *Spectacular Girls*, 5.
13. Mathieson, "Viewer Society."; Dubrofsky and Wood, "Posting Racism and Sexism."

14. Halliday, Buy Black, 108.
15. Dubrofsky and Wood, "Posting Racism and Sexism," 285.
16. Kelley, Yo Mama's Disfunktional, 24; hooks, We Real Cool, 61.
17. Gaunt, "YouTube, Twerking, & You," 253.
18. March, "Letter to Jatavia Johnson and Caresha Brownlee," 21; Durham, Cooper, Morris, "Stage Hip-Hop Feminism Built," 723–24.
19. March, "Letter to Jatavia Johnson and Caresha Brownlee," 21.
20. Payne, "Cardi B-Beyoncé Complex," 34.
21. Payne, "Cardi B-Beyoncé Complex," 35.
22. Hernandez, Aesthetics of Excess, 11.
23. Hernandez, Aesthetics of Excess, 12.
24. People, "Final Interview."
25. Obama, "Oprah's 2020 Vision Tour Visionaries."
26. Cox, Shapeshifters, 171.
27. Bradley, Chronicling Stankonia, 52.
28. Boylorn, "On Being at Home with Myself."
29. HRH the Duchess of Sussex, "HRH the Duchess of Sussex."

CHAPTER 3. LOVING FAST-TAILED GIRLS

1. Morris, Pushout, 34.
2. Cottom, Thick, 194.
3. Kendall, Hood Feminism, 47.
4. Trudy, "Fast Tailed Girls."
5. Halliday, "Black Girls' Feistiness as Everyday Resistance."
6. Bailey, Misogynoir Transformed, 1.
7. Candler, "Next to Nothing," 0:08:30.
8. Candler, "Next to Nothing," 0:17:44.
9. Candler, "Next to Nothing," 0:18:00.
10. Jewell, From Mammy to Miss America, 46–47.
11. Halliday, Black Girlhood Studies Collection.
12. Halliday, Black Girlhood Studies Collection, 6.
13. Halliday, Black Girlhood Studies Collection, 7–8.
14. Durham, Home with Hip Hop Feminism, 85.
15. Cooper, Eloquent Rage, 135.
16. Douglas, Sexuality and the Black Church, 36.
17. Douglas, Sexuality and the Black Church, 36.
18. Douglas, Sexuality and the Black Church, 35–36.
19. Lomax, Jezebel Unhinged, 33.
20. White, Fast Girls, 17.

21. White, *Fast Girls*, 17.
22. Scott, *Extravagant Abjection*, 4–5.
23. Richardson-Whitfield, "So Far," 0:00:14.
24. Richardson-Whitfield, "So Far," 0:01:12.
25. Richardson-Whitfield, "So Far," 0:01:36.
26. Mabry, "Far Too Long," 0:05:56.
27. Mabry, "Far Too Long," 0:06:18.
28. Cooper, *Eloquent Rage*, 119.
29. Cooper, *Eloquent Rage*, 119.
30. Perry, *Vexy Thing*, 23.
31. Baldwin, DeRogatis, and Mitchell, "On Behalf of the 48 Girls."
32. hampton, "Diddy Is 'Family over Everything.'" At the time of her documentary's release in early 2019, hampton herself authored Diddy's *Essence* Mother's Day cover story, rehabilitating his image.
33. Cottom, *Thick*, 12; Roach, "(Re)Turning to 'Rape.'"
34. Leung and Williams, "#MeToo and Intersectionality."
35. Baldwin, DeRogatis, and Mitchell, "On Behalf of the 48 Girls," 110.
36. Simmons, *Crescent City Girls*; Lomax, *Jezebel Unhinged*; Chatelain, *South Side Girls*.
37. Chatelain, *South Side Girls*, 87.
38. Hartman, *Wayward Lives*.
39. Chatelain, *South Side Girls*, 15.
40. Love, *Hip Hop's Li'l Sistas Speak*, 86.
41. Ford, *Dressed in Dreams*, 138–39.

CHAPTER 4. BLACK GIRLS SAVE THE WORLD

1. Taft, "Hopeful, Harmless, and Heroic."
2. Cox, *Shapeshifters*, 91.
3. Bernstein, *Racial Innocence*; Morris, *Pushout*; Shange, *Progressive Dystopia*.
4. McCarthy, "'Girl with All the Gifts' Behind the Scenes Featurette."
5. McCarthy, "'Girl with All the Gifts' Behind the Scenes Featurette."
6. Carey, *Girl with All the Gifts*, 1–2.
7. Carey, *Girl with All the Gifts*, 10.
8. Strings, *Fearing the Black Body*; Fleetwood, *Troubling Vision*; Hernandez, *Aesthetics of Excess*.
9. Webster, *Beyond the Boundaries of Childhood*.
10. Simmons, *Crescent City Girls*; Baumgartner, *In Pursuit of Knowledge*.

11. Ibrahim, *Black Age*, 16.
12. Perry, *Vexy Thing*, 23.
13. Gomer, *White Balance*, 164.
14. Gomer, *White Balance*, 190–91.
15. Warner, "Plastic Representation."
16. Warner, "Plastic Representation," n3.
17. King Watts, "Postracial Fantasies, Blackness, and Zombies."; Means Coleman, *Horror Noire*; Phillips and Witchard, *London Gothic*; Rogers, "Hostile Geographies."
18. Thomas, *Dark Fantastic*, 7.
19. Thomas, *Dark Fantastic*, 26.
20. Hall, *Essential Essays Vol. 1*, 309.
21. Thomas, *Dark Fantastic*, 56.
22. Breznican, "Sundance 2012"; Brox, "Monster of Representation"; Yaeger, "Beasts of the Southern Wild."
23. Hackett, "Racism of 'Beasts'"; Nyong'o, "Little Monsters."
24. Lukenbill, "Interview"; Denby, "Beasts of the Southern Wild"; Maclear, "Something So Broken."
25. Alibar, *Juicy and Delicious*, 6.
26. hooks, "No Love."
27. Breznican, "Sundance 2012."
28. Alibar, *Juicy and Delicious*, 8.
29. Alibar, *Juicy and Delicious*, 8.
30. Zeitlin, *Beasts*, 0:24:32.
31. Zeitlin, *Beasts*, 0:19:47, 0:33:10.
32. Zeitlin, *Beasts*, 0:13:09.
33. Zeitlin, *Beasts*, 0:18:52.
34. Zeitlin, *Beasts*, 0:17:30.
35. Zeitlin, *Beasts*, 1:04:15.
36. Epstein, Blake, and González, "Girlhood Interrupted"; Orenstein, *Cinderella Ate My Daughter*.
37. Denby, "Beasts of the Southern Wild."

CHAPTER 5. DISPENSABLE BLACK GIRLS

1. Procope Bell, "Pick-Me," 2–3.
2. Steele, *Digital Black Feminism*, 38.
3. Thomas, *Dark Fantastic*, 5–6.
4. hooks, *Feminist Theory*, 118.
5. Lindsey, "Let Me Blow Your Mind," 74.

6. Edwards, *Other Side of Terror*, 9.
7. Joost and Shulman, *Project Power*, 0:05:40.
8. Joost and Shulman, *Project Power*, 0:34:48.
9. Joost and Shulman, *Project Power*, 0:19:37.
10. Joost and Shulman, *Project Power*, 0:50:50.
11. Joost and Shulman, *Project Power*, 0:51:08.
12. Joost and Shulman, *Project Power*, 0:51:37.
13. Green et al., *Sociology of Cardi B*.
14. Joost and Shulman, *Project Power*, 0:53:40.
15. Joost and Shulman, *Project Power*, 0:56:52.
16. Joost and Shulman, *Project Power*, 0:59:27.
17. Joost and Shulman, *Project Power*, 01:03:01.
18. Joost and Shulman, *Project Power*, 01:11:36.
19. Joost and Shulman, *Project Power*, 01:34:43.
20. Joost and Shulman, *Project Power*, 01:36:00.
21. Joost and Shulman, *Project Power*, 01:41:07.
22. Joost and Shulman, *Project Power*, 01:43:11.
23. Joost and Shulman, *Project Power*, 0:54:49.
24. Halliday, *Buy Black*.
25. DuVernay, *Wrinkle in Time*, 0:05:31.
26. DuVernay, *Wrinkle in Time*, 0:07:22.
27. DuVernay, *Wrinkle in Time*, 0:08:01.
28. DuVernay, *Wrinkle in Time*, 1:01:40.
29. Morris, *Pushout*; Shange, *Progressive Dystopia*.
30. DuVernay, *Wrinkle in Time*, 0:06:55.
31. DuVernay, *Wrinkle in Time*, 0:27:50.
32. DuVernay, *Wrinkle in Time*, 1:29:46.

CHAPTER 6. MEAN (BLACK) GIRLS

1. Halliday, *Buy Black*.
2. Shange, *Progressive Dystopia*, 121.
3. Simmons, *Crescent City Girls*; Chatelain, *South Side Girls*; Hartman, *Wayward Lives*; Baumgartner, *In Pursuit of Knowledge*; Field et. al, "History of Black Girlhood."
4. Poe, *Selah and the Spades*, 1:07:14.
5. Poe, *Selah and the Spades*, 0:02:25.
6. Poe, *Selah and the Spades*, 0:02:28; Budds, "Origin Story of the 'Black Panther' Throne."

7. Morris, *Pushout*; Brown and Halliday, "Mid-Twerk and Mid-Laugh."
8. Poe, *Selah and the Spades*, 0:07:18.
9. Poe, *Selah and the Spades*, 0:07:49.
10. Poe, *Selah and the Spades*, 0:02:51.
11. Poe, *Selah and the Spades*, 0:48:09.
12. Poe, *Selah and the Spades*, 0:08:37.
13. Poe, *Selah and the Spades*, 0:20:22.
14. Doucouré, *Cuties*, 0:11:32.
15. "People Are up in Arms," *Bustle*.
16. Doucouré, *Cuties*, 0:12:31.
17. Doucouré, *Cuties*, 0:17:51.
18. Doucouré, *Cuties*, 0:40:24, 01:02:20.
19. Doucouré, *Cuties*, 1:09:55.
20. Doucouré, *Cuties*, 01:00:29, 01:01:56.
21. Doucouré, *Cuties*, 1:14:21.
22. Doucouré, *Cuties*, 1:16:25.

EPILOGUE. FINDING HEALING IN FAILURE

1. Lorde, *Sister Outsider*, 124.
2. Cineas, "Ma'Khia Bryant Shooting."
3. Jones, "Malcolm X."
4. Prince-Blythewood, *Woman King*, 30:14.
5. hooks, *Sisters of the Yam*, 7.
6. Lorde, *Cancer Journals*, 38.
7. Lorde, *Cancer Journals*, 66.
8. Lorde, *Cancer Journals*, 66.
9. Lorde, *Cancer Journals*, 59.
10. Lorde, *Cancer Journals*, 40.
11. Lorde *Cancer Journals*, 62, 63.

BIBLIOGRAPHY

Alibar, Lucy. *Juicy and Delicious: The Play That Inspired the Motion Picture "Beasts of the Southern Wild."* New York: Diversion Books, 2013.

Amber, Jeannine. "No Ordinary Love: Sean 'Diddy' Combs and Kim Porter." *Essence*, December 16, 2009. https://www.essence.com/newsf/no-ordinary-love-sean-diddy-combs-and-ki/.

Bailey, Moya. *Misogynoir Transformed: Black Women's Digital Resistance.* New York: New York University Press, 2021.

Baldwin, Sheila V., Jim DeRogatis, and Mary A. Mitchell. "On Behalf of the 48 Girls: The DeRogatis/Mitchell R. Kelly Interviews." *Journal of Black Sexuality and Relationships* 5, no. 4 (2019): 99–113. https://doi.org/10.1353/bsr.2019.0011.

Baumgartner, Kabria. *In Pursuit of Knowledge: Black Women and Educational Activism in Antebellum America.* New York: New York University Press, 2019.

Benbow, Candice. "4:43." Candice Marie Benbow, November 11, 2018. https://candicebenbow.com/blog/443.

Bernstein, Robin. *Racial Innocence: Performing American Childhood from Slavery to Civil Rights.* New York: New York University Press, 2011.

Beyoncé. *Lemonade.* Parkwood Entertainment, Sony Music, 2016.

Boffone, Trevor. *Renegades: Digital Dance Cultures from Dubsmash to TikTok.* New York: Oxford University Press, 2021.

Boylorn, Robin M. "On Being at Home with Myself: Blackgirl Autoethnography as Research Praxis." *International Review of Qualitative Research* 9, no. 1 (2016): 44–58. https://doi.org/10.1525/irqr.2016.9.1.44.

Bradley, Regina N. *Chronicling Stankonia: The Rise of the Hip Hop South.* Chapel Hill: University of North Carolina Press, 2021.

Breznican, Anthony. "Sundance 2012: 'Beasts of the Southern Wild' Introduces Funny, Fearsome Cutie-pie." *Entertainment Weekly*, January 29, 2012. https://ew.com/article/2012/01/29/sundance-beasts-of-the-southern-wild/.

Brogan, Jacob. "This Obscene Insult Is Suddenly Everywhere. But Does Anyone Know What It Means?" *Slate*, August 18, 2015. https://slate.com/human-interest/2015/08/what-does-fuckboy-mean.html.

Brown, August. "Sean 'Diddy' Combs Sexual Harassment Suit Includes Notable Music Industry Names." *Los Angeles Times*, February 28, 2024. https://www.latimes.com/entertainment-arts/music/story/2024-02-28/diddy-lawsuit-sexual-harrassment-explainer.

Brown, Kara. "The Definition of 'Fuckboy' Is Not What Bad Trend Pieces Are Telling You." *Jezebel*, August 21, 2015. https://jezebel.com/the-definition-of-fuckboy-is-not-what-bad-trend-pieces-1725157828.

Brown, Ruth Nicole. *Black Girlhood Celebration: Toward a Hip-Hop Feminist Pedagogy*. New York: Peter Lang, 2008.

Brown, Ruth Nicole, and Aria S. Halliday. "Mid-Twerk and Mid-Laugh." In *Investing in the Educational Success of Black Women and Girls*, edited by Lori D. Patton, Venus E. Evans-Winters, and Charlotte E. Jacobs, 39–56. Sterling, VA: Stylus Publishing, 2022.

Brox, Ali. "The Monster of Representation: Climate Change and Magical Realism in Beasts of the Southern Wild." *Journal of the Midwest Modern Language Association* 49, no. 1 (2016): 139–55. https://doi.org/10.1353/mml.2016.0015.

Bryant, Kimberly. "Black Girls Code." Speech. TEDxKC, Kansas City, October 5, 2013. YouTube video, 15:02. https://www.youtube.com/watch?v=TJ-m47CxAI0.

Budds, Diana. "The Origin Story of the 'Black Panther' Throne." *Curbed*, February 20, 2018. https://archive.curbed.com/2018/2/20/17032838/black-panther-wakanda-throne-peacock-chair.

Bustle. "People Are up in Arms over This New Netflix Movie without Having Seen It." September 16, 2020. https://www.bustle.com/entertainment/netflix-cuties-controversy-explained.

Butler, Tamara. "Black Girl Cartography: Black Girlhood and Place-Making in Education Research." *Review of Research in Education* 42, no. 1 (2018): 28–45. https://doi.org/10.3102/0091732X187762114.

Candler, Kat, dir. *Queen Sugar*. Season 1, episode 9, "Next to Nothing." Aired November 2, 2016, on Oprah Winfrey Network (OWN). Hulu.

Carey, M. R. *The Girl with All the Gifts*. London: Orbit Books, 2014.

Chatelain, Marcia. *South Side Girls: Growing Up in the Great Migration.* Durham, NC: Duke University Press, 2015.

Cineas, Fabiola. "The Ma'Khia Bryant Shooting and Black Girls' Invisible Fight against Police Violence." *Vox*, May 1, 2021. https://www.vox.com/22406055/makhia-bryant-police-shooting-columbus-ohio.

Cooper, Brittney. "A'n't I a Lady?: Race Women, Michelle Obama, and the Ever-Expanding Democratic Imagination." *MELUS* 35, no. 4 (2010): 39–57.

———. *Eloquent Rage: A Black Feminist Discovers Her Superpower.* New York: St. Martin's, 2018.

Cottom, Tressie McMillan. *Thick: And Other Essays.* New York: New Press, 2019.

Cox, Aimee Meredith. *Shapeshifters: Black Girls and the Choreography of Citizenship.* Durham, NC: Duke University Press, 2015.

Davis, Rachaell. "New Study Shows Black Women Are among the Most Educated in U.S." *Essence*, October 27, 2020. https://www.essence.com/news/new-study-black-women-most-educated/.

Denby, David. "Beasts of the Southern Wild." *New Yorker*, June 29, 2012. https://www.newyorker.com/culture/culture-desk/beasts-of-the-southern-wild.

Doucouré, Maïmouna, dir. *Cuties.* Paris: Zangro, 2020. Netflix.

Douglas, Kelly Brown. *Sexuality and the Black Church: A Womanist Perspective.* Maryknoll, NY: Orbis Books, 1999.

Dubrofsky, Rachel E., and Megan M. Wood. "Posting Racism and Sexism: Authenticity, Agency and Self-Reflexivity in Social Media." *Communication & Critical/Cultural Studies* 11, no. 3 (2014): 282–87. https://doi.org/10.1080/14791420.2014.926247.

Durham, Aisha. *Home with Hip Hop Feminism: Performances in Communication and Culture.* New York: Peter Lang, 2014.

Durham, Aisha, Brittney C. Cooper, and Susana M. Morris. "The Stage Hip-Hop Feminism Built: A New Directions Essay." *Signs* 38, no. 3 (2013): 721–37. https://doi.org/10.1086/668843.

DuVernay, Ava, dir. *A Wrinkle in Time.* Burbank, CA: Walt Disney Pictures, 2018. Disney+.

Edwards, Erica R. *The Other Side of Terror: Black Women and the Culture of US Empire.* New York: New York University Press, 2021.

Epstein, Rebecca, Jamilia Blake, and Thalia González. "Girlhood Interrupted: The Erasure of Black Girls' Childhood." SSRN. June 27, 2017. http://dx.doi.org/10.2139/ssrn.3000695.

Essence. "Kim Porter on Breaking Up with Sean 'Diddy' Combs and Starting Fresh." December 16, 2009. https://www.essence.com/news/kim-porter-on-breaking-up-with-sean-didd/.

Field, Corinne T., Tammy-Charelle Owens, Marcia Chatelain, Lakisha Simmons, Abosede George, and Rhian Keyse. "The History of Black Girlhood: Recent Innovations and Future Directions." *Journal of the History of Childhood and Youth* 9, no. 3. (2016): 383–401. https://doi.org/10.1353/hcy.2016.0067.

Fleetwood, Nicole R. *Troubling Vision: Performance, Visuality, and Blackness.* Chicago: University of Chicago Press, 2011.

Ford, Tanisha C. *Dressed in Dreams: A Black Girl's Love Letter to the Power of Fashion.* New York: St. Martin's, 2019.

Gaunt, Kyra D. *The Games Black Girls Play: Learning the Ropes from Double-Dutch to Hip-Hop.* New York: New York University Press, 2006.

———. "YouTube, Twerking and You: Context Collapse and the Handheld Co-Presence of Black Girls and Miley Cyrus." *Journal of Popular Music Studies* 27, no. 3 (2015): 244–73. https://doi.org/10.1111/jpms.12130.

Gomer, Justin. *White Balance: How Hollywood Shaped Colorblind Ideology and Undermined Civil Rights.* Chapel Hill: University of North Carolina Press, 2020.

Gonzalez, Eddie. "Jay-Z's '4:44' Humanizes Him through Fatherhood, Therapy and Infidelity." UPROXX, July 3, 2017. https://uproxx.com/music/jay-z-shawn-carter-444/.

Green, Aaryn, Maretta Darnell McDonald, Veronica A. Newton, Candice C. Robinson, and Shantee Rosado. *The Sociology of Cardi B: A Trap Feminist Approach.* New York: Routledge, 2025.

Hackett, Thomas. "The Racism of 'Beasts of the Southern Wild.'" *New Republic*, February 19, 2013. https://newrepublic.com/article/112407/racism-beasts-southern-wild.

Hall, Stuart. *Essential Essays: Identity and Diaspora Vol. 1.* Edited by David Morley. Durham, NC: Duke University Press, 2019.

Halliday, Aria S., ed. *The Black Girlhood Studies Collection.* Toronto: Women's Press, 2019.

———. "Black Girls' Feistiness as Everyday Resistance in Toni Cade Bambara's: Gorilla, My Love." *Palimpsest: A Journal on Women, Gender, and the Black International* 9, no. 1 (2020): 50–64. https://doi.org/10.1353/pal.2020.0012.

———. *Buy Black: How Black Women Transformed US Pop Culture.* Urbana: University of Illinois Press, 2022.

———. "Miley, What's Good?" *Girlhood Studies* 11, no. 3 (2018): 67–83. https://doi.org/10.3167/ghs.2018.110307.

———. "Trauma and the Formation of Radical Black Girl Subjectivity in Nalo Hopkinson's *Midnight Robber*." *Women, Gender, and Families of Color* 11, no. 1 (2023): 27–48. https://doi.org/10.5406/23260947.11.1.02.

Halliday, Aria S., and Nadia E. Brown. "The Power of Black Girl Magic Anthems: Nicki Minaj, Beyoncé, and 'Feeling Myself' as Political Empowerment." *Souls* 20, no. 2 (2018): 222–38. https://doi.org/10.1080/10999949.2018.1520067.

Halliday, Aria S., and Ashley N. Payne. "Twenty-First Century B.I.T.C.H. Frameworks: Hip Hop Feminism Comes of Age." *Journal of Hip Hop Studies* 7, no. 1 (2020): 8–18.

hampton, dream. "Diddy Is 'Family over Everything' after the Death of Kim Porter." *Essence*, April 23, 2019. https://www.essence.com/feature/diddy-family-over-everything-after-death-kim-porter/.

Hartman, Saidiya. *Wayward Lives, Beautiful Experiments: Intimate Histories of Social Upheaval.* New York: W. W. Norton, 2019.

Hernandez, Jillian. *Aesthetics of Excess: The Art and Politics of Black and Latina Embodiment.* Durham, NC: Duke University Press, 2020.

Hill, DaMaris B. *Breath Better Spent: Living Black Girlhood.* New York: Bloomsbury, 2022.

hooks, bell. *Black Looks: Race and Representation.* Boston: South End Press, 1992.

———. *Feminist Theory: From Margin to Center.* Boston: South End Press, 1984.

———. "No Love in the Wild." *NewBlackMan (in Exile)*, September 5, 2012. https://www.newblackmaninexile.net/2012/09/bell-hooks-no-love-in-wild.html.

———. *Sisters of the Yam: Black Women and Self-Recovery.* 2nd ed. New York: Routledge, 2014.

———. *We Real Cool: Black Men and Masculinity.* New York: Routledge, 2003.

HRH the Duchess of Sussex. "HRH the Duchess of Sussex Interviews Michelle Obama in the September Issue." *British Vogue*, July 29, 2019. https://www.vogue.co.uk/article/michelle-obama-duchess-of-sussex-interview-2019.

Ibrahim, Habiba. *Black Age: Oceanic Lifespans and the Time of Black Life*. New York: New York University Press, 2021.

Iton, Richard. *In Search of the Black Fantastic: Politics and Popular Culture in the Post-Civil Rights Era*. Oxford: Oxford University Press, 2010.

Jay-Z. *4:44*. ROC Nation, UMG Recordings, 2017.

Jewell, K. Sue. *From Mammy to Miss America and Beyond: Cultural Images and the Shaping of US Social Policy*. New York: Routledge, 1993.

Jones, Feminista. "Malcolm X Stood Up for Black Women When Few Others Would." ZORA, August 7, 2020. https://zora.medium.com/malcolm-x-stood-up-for-black-women-when-few-others-would-68e8b2ea2747.

Joost, Henry, and Ariel Schulman, dirs. *Project Power*. New York: Screen Arcade, 2020. Netflix.

Kelley, Robin. *Yo Mama's Disfunktional: Fighting the Culture Wars in Urban America*. New York: Beacon, 1998.

Kendall, Mikki. *Hood Feminism: Notes from the Women That a Movement Forgot*. New York: Penguin, 2020.

Kenny, Lorraine, ed. *Daughters of Suburbia: Growing Up White, Middle Class, and Female*. New Brunswick, NJ: Rutgers University Press, 2000.

Khoja-Moolji, Shenila. *Forging the Ideal Educated Girl: The Production of Desirable Subjects in Muslim South Asia*. Oakland: University of California Press, 2018.

Letterman, David. *My Next Guest Needs No Introduction with David Letterman*. Season 1, episode 4, "I Had a Paper Route Too." Aired April 6, 2018, on Netflix.

Leung, Rebecca, and Robert Williams. "#MeToo and Intersectionality: An Examination of the #MeToo Movement through the R. Kelly Scandal." *Journal of Communication Inquiry* 43, no. 4 (2019): 349–71. https://doi.org/10.1177/0196859919874138.

Lindsey, Treva B. *America, Goddam: Violence, Black Women, and the Struggle for Justice*. Oakland: University of California Press, 2022.

———. "Let Me Blow Your Mind: Hip Hop Feminist Futures in Theory and Praxis." *Urban Education* 50, no. 1 (2015): 52–77. https://doi.org/10.1177/0042085914563184.

Lomax, Tamura A. *Jezebel Unhinged: Loosing the Black Female Body in Religion and Culture*. Durham, NC: Duke University Press, 2018.

Lorde, Audre. *The Cancer Journals*. Special ed. San Francisco: aunt lute books, 1997.

———. *Sister Outsider: Essays and Speeches*. Berkeley, CA: Crossing Press, 1984.

Love, Bettina L. *Hip Hop's Li'l Sistas Speak: Negotiating Hip Hop Identities and Politics in the New South*. New York: Peter Lang, 2012.

Lukenbill, Mark. "Interview: Oscar Nominee Lucy Alibar on Meeting Tony Kushner, Working with Guillermo Del Toro, and Life after 'Beasts.'" *IndieWire*, March 12, 2013. https://www.indiewire.com/2013/03/interview-oscar-nominee-lucy-alibar-on-meeting-tony-kushner-working-with-guillermo-del-toro-and-life-after-beasts-40237/.

Mabry, Tina, dir. *Queen Sugar*. Season 1, episode 12, "Far Too Long." Aired November 23, 2016, on Oprah Winfrey Network (OWN). Hulu.

Maclear, Kyo. "Something So Broken: Black Care in the Wake of *Beasts of the Southern Wild*." *ISLE: Interdisciplinary Studies in Literature and Environment* 25, no. 3 (2018): 603–29. https://doi.org/10.1093/isle/isy060.

Mans, Jasmine. *Black Girl, Call Home*. New York: Berkley, 2021.

March, Kyra. "Letter to Jatavia Johnson and Caresha Brownlee (The City Girls)." *Journal of Hip Hop Studies* 7, no. 1 (2020): 19–25.

Mathieson, Thomas. "The Viewer Society: Michel Foucault's 'Panopticon' Revisited." *Theoretical Criminology* 1, no. 2 (1997): 215–34.

McCarthy, Colm. "'The Girl with All the Gifts' Behind the Scenes Featurette." YouTube video, 19:54. Posted by Flicks and the City Clips, September 8, 2016. https://www.youtube.com/watch?v=2BgbfH5iaqY.

Means Coleman, Robin R. *Horror Noire: Blacks in American Horror Films from the 1890s to Present*. New York: Routledge, 2011.

Morgan, Joan. *When Chickenheads Come Home to Roost: A Hip-Hop Feminist Breaks It Down*. New York: Simon and Schuster, 1999.

Morris, Monique. *Pushout: The Criminalization of Black Girls in Schools*. New York: New Press, 2016.

Neal, Mark Anthony. *Looking for Leroy: Illegible Black Masculinities*. New York: New York University Press, 2013.

Noble, Safiya Umoja. *Algorithms of Oppression: How Search Engines Reinforce Racism*. New York: New York University Press, 2018.

Nyong'o, Tavia. "Little Monsters: Race, Sovereignty, and Queer Inhumanism in Beasts of the Southern Wild." *GLQ: A Journal of Lesbian and Gay Studies* 21, no. 2–3 (2015): 249–72. https://doi.org/10.1215/10642684-2843335.

Obama, Michelle. "Oprah's 2020 Vision Tour Visionaries: Michelle Obama Interview." Interview by Oprah Winfrey. YouTube video, 53:20. Posted by WeightWatchers, February 12, 2020. https://www.youtube.com/watch?v=XvFaaO5b4hE.

Orenstein, Peggy. *Cinderella Ate My Daughter: Dispatches from the Front Lines of the New Girlie-Girl Culture*. New York: Harper Paperbacks, 2012.

Oware, Matthew. "Decent Daddy, Imperfect Daddy: Black Male Rap Artists' Views of Fatherhood and the Family." *Journal of African American Studies* 15, no. 3 (2011): 327–51. https://doi.org/10.1007/s12111-010-9155-9.

Payne, Ashley N. "The Cardi B-Beyoncé Complex: Ratchet Respectability and Black Adolescent Girlhood." *Journal of Hip Hop Studies* 7, no. 1 (2020): 19–25.

Penn, Charli. "Diddy and Daughters Grace the Cover of Essence as He Opens Up about Loving and Losing Kim Porter." *Essence*, April 23, 2019. https://www.essence.com/love/diddy-daughters-essence-cover-loving-losing-kim-porter/.

People. "The Final Interview with the Obamas." YouTube video, 27:11. Posted by People, December 20, 2016. https://www.youtube.com/watch?v=iH1ZJVqJO3Y.

Perry, Imani. *Vexy Thing: On Gender and Liberation*. Durham, NC: Duke University Press, 2018.

Phillips, Lawrence, and Anne Witchard, eds. *London Gothic: Place, Space and the Gothic Imagination*. London: Bloomsbury Publishing, 2012.

Poe, Tayarisha, dir. *Selah and the Spades*. Malibu, CA: Argent Pictures, 2019. Amazon Prime Video.

Pough, Gwendolyn D. *Check It While I Wreck It: Black Womanhood, Hip-Hop Culture, and the Public Sphere*. Boston: Northeastern University Press, 2004.

Prince-Blythewood, Gina, dir. *The Woman King*. Burbank, CA: TriStar Pictures, 2022. Netflix.

Procope Bell, Danielle. "'Pick-Me' Black Women: Tactical Patriarchal Femininity in the Black Manosphere." *Feminist Media Studies*, October (2023): 1–19. https://doi.org/10.1080/14680777.2023.2262163.

Projansky, Sarah. *Spectacular Girls: Media Fascination and Celebrity Culture*. New York: New York University Press, 2014.

Richardson-Whitfield, Salli, dir. *Queen Sugar*. Season 1, episode 10, "So Far." Aired November 9, 2016, on Oprah Winfrey Network (OWN). Hulu.

Roach, Shoniqua. "(Re)Turning to 'Rape and the Inner Lives of Black Women': A Black Feminist Forum on the Culture of Dissemblance." *Signs: Journal of Women in Culture and Society* 45, no. 3 (2020): 515–19. https://doi.org/10.1086/706429.

Rogers, Dehanza. "Hostile Geographies: Black Girls Fight to Save Themselves and the World." *Girlhood Studies* 15, no. 1 (2022): 34–49. https://doi.org/10.3167/ghs.2022.150104.

Rose, Tricia. *Black Noise: Rap Music and Black Culture in Contemporary America*. Hanover, NH: Wesleyan, 1994.

Scott, Darieck. *Extravagant Abjection: Blackness, Power, and Sexuality in the African American Literary Imagination*. New York: New York University Press, 2010.

Shange, Savannah. *Progressive Dystopia: Abolition, Anthropology, and Race in the New San Francisco*. Durham, NC: Duke University Press, 2019.

Shepherd, Julianne Escobedo. "A Brief Taxonomy of the Fuccboi (RIP)." *Jezebel*, September 26, 2014. https://jezebel.com/a-brief-taxonomy-of-the-fuccboi-rip-1638331191.

Simmons, LaKisha Michelle. *Crescent City Girls: The Lives of Young Black Women in Segregated New Orleans*. Chapel Hill: University of North Carolina Press, 2015.

Smith, Jada Pinkett. "Rapper T.I. and His Wife Tiny Set the Record Straight." *Red Table Talk*, Facebook, November 25, 2019. Video, 22:24. https://www.facebook.com/watch/?v=1803664559768440.

———. "T.I. and Tiny: Back from the Brink of Divorce (Part 2)." *Red Table Talk*, Facebook, December 2, 2019. Video, 28:15. https://www.facebook.com/watch/?v=2795208257198749.

Steele, Catherine Knight. *Digital Black Feminism*. New York: New York University Press, 2021.

Strings, Sabrina. *Fearing the Black Body: The Racial Origins of Fat Phobia*. New York: New York University Press, 2019.

Taft, Jessica K. "Hopeful, Harmless, and Heroic." *Girlhood Studies* 13, no. 2 (2020): 1–17. https://doi.org/10.3167/ghs.2020.130203.

Tanenbaum, Leora. *Slut! Growing Up Female with a Bad Reputation*. New York: Harper Perennial, 2000.

Thomas, Ebony Elizabeth. *The Dark Fantastic: Race and the Imagination from Harry Potter to the Hunger Games*. New York: New York University Press, 2019.

Tillet, Salamishah. "Make Revolution Irresistible: The Role of the Cultural Worker in the Twenty-First Century." *PMLA: Publications of the Modern Language Association of America* 130, no. 2 (2015): 481–87.

Tounsel, Timeka. *Branding Black Womanhood: Media Citizenship from Black Power to Black Girl Magic.* New Brunswick, NJ: Rutgers University Press, 2022.

Trudy. "Fast Tailed Girls: Examining the Stereotypes and Abuse That Black Girls Face." *Gradient Lair*, December 30, 2015. http://www.gradientlair.com/post/68646097154/fast-tailed-girls-stereotyped-abused-black-girls.

Valdivia, Angharad N. "Living in a Hybrid Material World: Girls, Ethnicity and Mediated Doll Products." *Girlhood Studies* 2, no. 1 (2009): 73–93.

Vidal, Juan. "An Ode to Jay-Z, The Ultimate Rap Dad." *Vibe*, June 16, 2019. https://www.vibe.com/2019/06/an-ode-to-jay-z-the-ultimate-rap-dad.

Warner, Kristen J. "Plastic Representation." *Film Quarterly* 71, no. 2 (2017). https://filmquarterly.org/2017/12/04/in-the-time-of-plastic-representation/.

Watts, Eric King. "Postracial Fantasies, Blackness, and Zombies." *Communication and Critical/Cultural Studies* 14, no. 4 (2017): 317–33. https://doi.org/10.1080/14791420.2017.1338742.

Webster, Crystal Lynn. *Beyond the Boundaries of Childhood: African American Children in the Antebellum North.* Chapel Hill: University of North Carolina Press, 2021.

White, Emily. *Fast Girls: Teenage Tribes and the Myth of the Slut.* New York: Simon and Schuster, 2002.

Yaeger, Patricia. "Beasts of the Southern Wild and Dirty Ecology." *Southern Spaces*, February 13, 2013. https://southernspaces.org/2013/beasts-southern-wild-and-dirty-ecology/.

Zeitlin, Benh, dir. *Beasts of the Southern Wild.* Montegut, LA: Court13, 2012. Hulu.

INDEX

abuse: of Black girls, 16–18, 20–21, 25, 65, 84, 148; physical, 37, 41, 156–57; protection of abusers, 2, 69, 158–60, 159–160; sexual, 37, 61, 80–82, 86, 154. See also sexual assault; violence
activism, political, 13, 15, 85–86, 97, 106
adultification, 20, 63–65, 68, 89, 100, 120, 131
aesthetics of excess, 55
Alex (Wrinkle in Time character), 121–26
algorithms, online, 2–3, 47–48, 51, 55
Alibar, Lucy, 99; Juicy and Delicious, 99. See also Beasts of the Southern Wild
Amazon Prime, 18, 60, 146
Amy (Cuties character): emotional safety of, 142–43, 148, 153; hypervisibility and, 151; as mean girl, 20, 128, 130–31, 149; story of, 137–42
Angelica (Cuties character), 138–41
assimilation, 14, 44, 115, 124–25, 127, 130
Atlanta, GA, 2, 40, 72, 80
authenticity, 11, 17, 25, 51, 152

Bad Boy Records, 36–37
Baldwin, Sheila, 81
Banfield-Norris, Adrienne, 10, 38
Banks, Erica, 50; "Buss It," 50
Baszile, Natalie, 74; Queen Sugar (book), 74
Baumgartner, Kabria, 92–93

Beasts of the Southern Wild (film), 19, 86, 99–106, 121. See also Hushpuppy; Wink
Benbow, Candice Marie, 30–32; Red Lip Theology, 161
Beyoncé, 23–24, 29–30, 34, 39; "'03 Bonnie and Clyde," 29; "Daddy Lessons," 24; Lemonade, 24, 29
Black boys and men: and assault of Black girls and women, 80–82; emotional maturation of, 29–33, 41, 155; focus on, 4–7, 45; and hip-hop, 17, 23–29, 37, 39–41; murders of, 7, 45; and patriarchal power, 78. See also fatherhood; fuckboys; masculinity; patriarchy
Black Church, 71, 78. See also Christianity
Black feminism, 7–8, 18, 20, 68, 108, 147
Black girlhood: and activism, 86; and fast girls, 63, 65, 83; in film, 87; and hip-hop's daughters, 25; and hypervisibility, 44, 46, 52; overview of, 7–8, 68–69, 104–5, 146; in popular culture, 2–3; Southern, 58, 69–74
Black girls. See daughters; disposability of Black girls; fast girls; film, Black girls in; hypersexuality of Black girls and women; hypervisibility of Black girls and women; mean girls; saviors, Black girls as
Black Girls Code, 12–16

Black Girls Rock!, 12–16
Black Lives Matter, 7
Black men. See Black boys and men
blackness: and fast girls, 66, 73, 84;
  in film, 88, 92–93, 96, 129, 146; and
  hypervisibility, 17, 43, 46–47, 51
Black violability, 109–10
Black women: and Black girlhood, 7–8,
  68, 146, 155; in Black media, 9–11;
  community organizing of, 12–16;
  and Diddy, 17, 25, 33–37, 40–41;
  failing of, 5–7; and fastness, 69–74,
  78, 82; and fuckboys, 25–29; healing
  of, 148–52, 155; as hip-hop artists,
  54, 115; and hypervisibility, 17,
  43–45, 47, 49–54, 57–58; and Jay Z,
  17, 23–25, 29–33, 40–41; representations of Black girls by, 3, 65, 74, 79,
  129–30, 142; and T.I., 17, 25, 37–41;
  violence against, 7, 83, 109–10, 146,
  158. See also motherhood
Bland, Sandra, 7
Bond, Beverly, 14–15
boys. See Black boys and men
Bradford, Joy Harden, 161
Bradley, Regina, 58
Breakfast Club, The (radio show), 9–12
Brim, Misa Hylton, 33
Brown, Michael, 6, 45
Brown, Ruth Nicole, 52
Bryant, Kimberly, 13–15
Bryant, Ma'Khia, 146
Bryant, Thema, 161
bullying, 121–25, 131, 139–40, 153.
  See also mean girls
Butler, Tamara, 4

capitalism, 27–28, 32, 33, 37, 47, 150, 156
carcerality, 47, 48, 89. See also
  incarceration
Cardi B, 40, 54, 115
Carey, Mike, 87, 90–91, 96. See also
  Girl with All the Gifts, The
Carter, Blue Ivy, 23, 30

Carter, Shawn. See Jay Z
Carters, 30; Everything Is Love, 30
Cassie (singer), 33, 34, 37
celebrity, 8–9, 11, 47, 50–52
Chapman, Sarah, 33, 34, 36
Charlamagne tha God, 9–10
Chicago, IL, 43, 57, 80
Chika (rapper), 115
childhood, 38, 48, 63–64, 75, 92–93
Christianity, 18, 39, 69–74, 78–79,
  82–84. See also Eve; Jezebel trope
City Girls (rap group), 53–55; "Pussy
  Talk," 54; "Twerk," 54, 55
Collins, Patricia Hill, 68
colorblind casting: in Beasts of the
  Southern Wild, 100–101; in The Girl
  with All the Gifts, 89–92, 94–97;
  in A Wrinkle in Time, 122
colorblindness, 48, 89–90, 94–95, 97, 109
Color Purple, The (film), 63
Combs, Chance, 33, 34
Combs, Christian, 33, 34
Combs, Shawn. See Diddy
common sense, 97, 109, 154, 155, 157
context collapse, 48, 52
Cooper, Brittney, 70–73, 78; Eloquent
  Rage, 161
Copeny, Amariyanna "Little Miss
  Flint," 85–86, 106
Cottom, Tressie McMillan, 63, 64,
  71–72, 80
COVID-19 pandemic, 53
Cox, Aimee Meredith, 49, 57
Crenshaw, Kimberlé, 7
Cuties (film), 20, 128, 130–31, 137–42, 143.
  See also Amy; Angelica

dark fantastic, 96–97
daughters: and Diddy, 17, 34–37, 41;
  and healing, 152; and Jay Z, 17,
  23–25, 30–32, 41; and the Obamas,
  44, 47, 56–57, 59–60; in Project
  Power, 114–20; in Selah and the
  Spades, 133; and T.I., 17, 37–39, 41

Davis, Jordan, 45
Davis, Viola, 161; *Finding Me*, 161
Diddy, 17, 25, 29, 32, 33–37, 40–41, 158, 168n32; *Press Play*, 36
Diddy+7 (TV show), 37
Disney, 121, 122; Disney+ (streaming service), 18, 121, 133–34, 146
disposability of Black girls, 3–4, 18–19, 107–8, 143–44, 146, 149, 155; and fast girls, 63; in film, 87, 109–17, 120, 127–28; and mean girls, 87, 130–31
DJ Envy, 9–10
Douglas, Kelly Brown, 71, 73
Durham, Aisha, 71–73
DuVernay, Ava, 65–66, 74–75, 77, 122, 129
dystopias, 18–19, 31, 86–89, 93, 94, 98, 152. See also *Beasts of the Southern Wild*; *Girl with All the Gifts, The*

education, 4, 8, 12, 45, 52, 69, 85–86, 93; in *Project Power*, 111–12, 116, 120; in *Queen Sugar*, 76–77; in *Selah and the Spades*, 131–33; in *A Wrinkle in Time*, 123–25. See also bullying
Edwards, Erica, 110
embodied objectification, 129
emotional safety of Black girls, 64, 131, 137, 142–43
empathy, 87, 88, 90, 94
environmental justice, 85–86
Essence magazine, 33–37, 168n32
Evans-Winters, Venus, 52
Eve (biblical figure), 70–71

Facebook, 9–10, 14, 38, 48
failure of Black girls, 2–8, 16–21, 84, 86, 147–48, 155–60
family, ideologies of, 4–6
Family Hustle, The (reality show), 37–38
fantastical realism, 18, 109, 122, 127
fast girls: definition of, 18, 49, 63–65, 82–84; and hip-hop's daughters, 25, 30; and the Obama girls, 41, 44, 45;

on *Queen Sugar*, 65–69, 75–79, 148; and R. Kelly, 79–82; in *Selah and the Spades*, 131, 135–36; in the South, 69–73. See also fast-tailed girls; hypersexuality; sluts
fast-tailed girls, 16, 18, 73, 76, 78, 84; definition of, 64–65
fatherhood: in the author's life, 156–57; in *Beasts of the Southern Wild*, 99–105; in *Cuties*, 138, 140–41; and hip-hop, 17, 24–25, 28–41; in *Project Power*, 114–20; in *Queen Sugar*, 66, 78–79; role in Black family, 5–6, 129–31; in *Selah and the Spades*, 133, 135, 137; in *A Wrinkle in Time*, 121–24
feminism: Black, 7–8, 18, 20, 68, 108, 147; hip-hop, 53–54; ratchet, 54
film, Black girls in, 15, 18–19, 84, 86–87, 108–9, 129–31, 143, 146, 152–53. See also disposability of Black girls; mean girls; saviors, Black girls as films. See titles of specific films
Fishback, Dominique, 60, 111
Flint, MI, 85, 106
Floyd, George, 9
Ford, Tanisha, 83; *Dressed in Dreams*, 161
France, 130, 137
Frank (*Project Power* character), 111, 114, 116–17, 119
fuckboys, 26–29, 33, 35, 37, 38, 40–41, 108

Gatin, Cammie, 90
Gaunt, Kyra, 48, 52–53
girlhood. See Black girlhood
girls. See daughters; disposability of Black girls; fast girls; film, Black girls in; hypersexuality of Black girls and women; hypervisibility of Black girls and women; mean girls; saviors, Black girls as
Girl with All the Gifts, The (Carey), 89–92, 94–98

INDEX 185

Girl with All the Gifts, The (film), 19, 86–99, 101, 106, 121. See also Justineau; Melanie
Google, 14, 47
Gomer, Justin, 94
Gray, Kishonna, 52

hair, 12, 45, 51, 53, 59, 83; in film, 104–5, 121–22, 125–27, 138–40
Hall, Stuart, 97
Halliday, Aria: Black Girlhood Studies Collection, The, 68–69; Buy Black, 51, 129; family of, 156–57; poem by, vii, 1
hampton, dream, 35–36, 80, 168n32; Surviving R. Kelly, 80
Harris, Clifford. See T.I.
Harris, Deyjah, 37–39
Harris, Tameka "Tiny," 37–39
Hartman, Saidiya, 49
healing, 20, 147, 148–55, 160
Hernandez, Jillian, 55
Hill, DaMaris B., 107, 145, 161
hip-hop: and Black girlhood, 58; daughters of, 17, 23–41, 133, 155; and feminism, 53–54; in Project Power, 112, 113, 115, 118, 120–21; talk shows, 8–12
Homecoming (podcast), 161
hooks, bell, 2; All About Love, 161; Feminist Theory, 109–10; review of Beasts of the Southern Wild, 100–101; Sisters of the Yam, 149–50
ho theology, 71
Houston, Whitney, 37, 156
Hulu, 37
Hushpuppy (Beasts of the Southern Wild character): colorblind casting of, 100–101; gender of, 104–5; healing and, 153; hypervisibility of, 151; as savior, 19, 86–87, 106, 148; story of, 99–104, 149
hypersexuality of Black girls and women, 48–50, 63–75, 80–81, 139. See also fast girls; fast-tailed girls; sluts
hypervisibility of Black girls and women, 16–17, 41, 47, 55, 61, 84, 131, 134–36, 148, 151. See also surveillance

Ibrahim, Habiba, 7, 93, 145
incarceration, 17, 27, 39, 40, 51, 74, 110. See also carcerality
infidelity, 24, 29–32, 39, 40
Instagram, 9, 33, 37, 48, 51, 67
integration, 45
Islam, 137–38, 141–42
Iton, Richard, 31

Jay Z: "'03 Bonnie and Clyde," 29; 4:44, 23, 29–30, 32, 36; "Beach Chair," 24; "Family Feud," 23; fatherhood and, 17, 25, 31–32, 37, 41; infidelities and, 29–31, 39; "Money, Cash, Hoes," 28
Jefferson, Atatiana, 7
Jewell, K. Sue, 68
Jezebel trope, 49, 54, 68, 71–73, 82
JLo, 33, 34
Johnson, Sheila, 161; Walk through Fire, 161
Jones, Nikki, 52
JT (rapper), 53–54
Juicy and Delicious (Alibar), 99. See also Beasts of the Southern Wild
Justineau (Girl with All the Gifts character), 88–89, 91, 94–98

Keke (Queen Sugar character): as fast girl, 65, 67–68, 75, 82–83, 129, 148, 149; healing and, 153; hypervisibility of, 151; story of, 66–67, 74, 76–79
Kelly, Robert (R.), 18, 80–81, 83, 158
King, Martin Luther, Jr., 44
Knowles-Carter, Beyoncé. See Beyoncé

Latinx people, 10, 55, 69, 74, 94
L'Engle, Madeline, 121; A Wrinkle in Time, 121–22, 153
Letterman, David, 31, 60

liberalism, 5, 6, 105, 114–15, 124. See also neoliberalism
Lindsey, Treva, 109–10
Locke, John, 5, 93
Lomax, Tamura, 71–72, 78
Lopez, Jennifer (JLo), 33, 34
Lorde, Audre: on failure, 158; on healing, 147–54; on the uses of anger, 145
Los Angeles, CA, 66, 74, 77

Major (Project Power character), 111–21, 124
Malcolm X, 40, 147
Mans, Jasmine, 4; Black Girl, Call Home, 161; "Missing Girls," 1–2
marriage, 31, 34, 37, 39, 51, 107–8, 138, 142
Martin, Trayvon, 6–7, 45
masculinity, 17, 19, 24–25, 28, 32, 43, 78, 108. See also fatherhood; fuckboys
McBride, Renisha, 7, 45, 146
mean girls, 122, 128–31, 148. See also Cuties; Selah and the Spades
Mean Girls (film), 129
Meg (Wrinkle in Time character): as disposable, 19, 108, 111, 127–28; healing and, 153; hypervisibility of, 151; as savior, 148; story of, 121–27
Megan Thee Stallion, 40–41, 43, 54, 60
Melanie (Girl with All the Gifts character): colorblind casting of, 89–97; healing and, 153; hypervisibility of, 151; as savior, 19, 86–87, 106, 148, 149; story of, 87–89, 98–99
men. See Black boys and men
Micah (Queen Sugar character), 66–68, 74–79, 153
Minaj, Nicki, 9, 51
miscarriages, 29, 30, 32, 37, 39
misogynoir: in Black media, 8–12; cultivation of, 4–8; definition of, 2–4, 154–55; and disposable Black girls, 115, 122, 124–25, 128; and fantastical realism, 18; and fast girls, 64, 66, 69, 75, 77, 82–83; healing from, 146–52, 155; in hip-hop, 17, 25, 31, 38, 39, 41; and hypervisibility, 17–18, 47, 54, 58, 61; and mean girls, 131, 137, 143; and salvific Black girls, 87
Morgan, Joan, 23, 24, 26; When Chickenheads Come Home to Roost, 23, 24, 26
Morris, Monique, 52, 89, 125
motherhood: in the author's life, 156–57; in Beasts of the Southern Wild, 103; in Cuties, 137–42, 153; and fast girls, 65, 70–71; in hip-hop, 36; and Michelle Obama, 45–46, 56–59; in Project Power, 111, 113–14, 120–21, 153; in Selah and the Spades, 133, 137, 142
Moynihan, Daniel Patrick, 4, 6, 12, 82
My Brother's Keeper program, 4–5, 7, 45

Nanua, Sennia, 88, 90, 92, 94
National Center for Education Statistics, 12, 45
Nawi (Woman King character), 149
Neal, Mark Anthony, 25; New Black Man, 161
neoliberalism, 50, 94, 95, 97, 114. See also colorblindness
Netflix, 18, 59, 143
Netflix and Chill, 76–77
New Orleans, LA, 1, 66, 99, 111, 113–14, 117, 127
New York, NY, 9, 29, 40
Noble, Safiya, 43, 47–48, 52

Obama, Barack: fatherhood and, 17, 52, 56, 59–60; presidency, 4–6, 12, 16, 43–46, 58, 85–86
Obama, Malia: hypervisibility of, 17–18, 41, 47, 52, 61, 148, 149, 151; media coverage of, 45–46, 59–60; in the White House, 43–45, 56–57
Obama, Michelle, 43–44, 46, 54, 56–57, 59–60; Becoming, 45, 57, 59; The Light We Carry, 59

INDEX 187

Obama, Sasha: hypervisibility of, 17–18, 41, 47, 52, 61, 148, 149, 151; on social media, 46, 48, 53–57, 60; in the White House, 43–45, 56
opacity of Black girls, 130–31
Oprah, 57, 65, 122, 125
Oprah Winfrey Network (OWN), 65
Oware, Matthew, 31

Paloma (*Selah and the Spades* character), 134–36, 142
Pandora, 90–93, 96, 98–99
patriarch. *See* fatherhood
patriarchal protection, 6, 107
patriarchy: and the Black family, 5–6, 41; and the disposability of Black girls, 107–8, 115, 117, 119; and fast girls, 70–71, 78–80, 83–84; and fuckboys, 27–29; healing from, 148, 155, 160
Payne, Ashley, 54–55
perfectionism, 127, 131–35
performances of nonrecognition, 27–28
Perry, Imani, 5, 27, 79
personhood, 5–6, 16, 27, 93
Pete, Megan. *See* Megan Thee Stallion
pick mes, 107–8
Pinkett-Smith, Jada, 10, 38–39
plastic representation, 95
police officers, 7, 51
popular culture, Black girls in, 2–4, 16, 65, 86, 129, 146, 147, 154. *See also* film, Black girls in
Porter, Kim, 33–37, 39
Prince-Blythewood, Gina, 149, 150. *See also Woman King, The*
Projansky, Sarah, 50
Project Power (film), 19, 108–21, 124, 127, 153. *See also* Frank; Major; Robin; Tracy
Public Enemy, 31–32
Puff Daddy. *See* Diddy

Queen Sugar (TV show), 65–69, 74–83, 122. *See also* Keke; Micah
queer people, 1, 10, 11

race-neutral casting. *See* colorblind casting
"race women," 17, 47
racism. *See* misogynoir; white supremacy
radio, 8–12
rap. *See* hip-hop
ratchedness, 50, 54–55
reality television, 37–38
Red Table Talk, 9–12, 38–39
Reid, Storm, 122
religion. *See* Christianity; Islam
representation: of Black girls, 2–4, 16, 20, 92, 155–56; of Black girls by Black women, 65, 75, 129, 142, 149; of Black girls in film, 87, 106, 109, 129–30, 143, 146; of Black girls in photographs, 49; of Black girls in tech, 14–15; of blackness, 17, 47; of the Obamas, 45; plastic, 95
respectability politics, 49, 54, 58, 68–69, 77–79, 82–83
Rice, Tamir, 45
R. Kelly, 18, 80–81, 83, 158
Robin (*Project Power* character) as disposable, 19, 108, 111, 127–28, 149; healing and, 153; hypervisibility of, 151; as savior, 148; story of, 111–21

Sapphires, 130
saviors, Black girls as, 18–19, 85–87, 108, 109, 148. *See also Beasts of the Southern Wild; Girl with All the Gifts, The*; white saviors
#SayHerName, 7
school. *See* education
Scott, Darieck, 73
Selah (*Selah and the Spades* character): emotional safety of, 142–43,

148; healing and, 153; hypervisibility of, 151; as mean girl, 20, 128, 130–31, 149; story of, 131–37, 141
Selah and the Spades (film), 20, 128, 130–37, 141, 143. See also Paloma; Selah
self-care. See healing
Senegal, 137–38
sexual assault, 37, 64, 80–82, 86, 154
sexuality of Black girls and women: in Black media, 9; and City Girls, 53–55; in *Cuties*, 138, 143; and the Obama girls, 17, 51, 54–58; online, 47–50; in the South, 69–74. See also fast girls; hypersexuality of Black girls and women
Shange, Savannah, 52, 89, 125, 130
Simmons, LaKisha, 92–93
slavery, 8, 49, 66, 92, 96, 110
sluts, 72–73, 82. See also fast girls
Snapchat, 46, 48, 51, 60
social media: and Black media, 8–12; comments on *Queen Sugar*, 67–68, 75–76, 79, 83; in *Cuties*, 139, 141, 153; and the Obamas, 45–46, 52–55, 57, 59–61; #SayHerName, 7; and surveillance, 18, 47–52, 159. See also *names of specific social media platforms*
South. See US South
Steele, Catherine Knight, 108
streaming services. See *names of specific services*
surveillance: of Black girls, 17–18, 61, 70, 85, 110, 147; in film, 84; of the Obamas, 18, 41, 46–47, 52, 55, 148; and social media, 18, 47–52, 159. See also hypervisibility of Black girls and women
Swarm (TV show), 60–61
synoptic premediated authenticity, 51

Taylor, Breonna, 9, 146
teacher films, 94
technology: Black girls and women in, 13–16; and surveillance, 47–52, 55
television. See *Queen Sugar*; reality television; *Swarm*
Therapy for Black Girls (podcast), 161
Thomas, Ebony Elizabeth, 48, 95–97, 109
Thompson, Cashawn, 14
T.I., 17, 25, 29, 32, 37–41
TikTok, 20, 46, 48–51, 53–55, 60
Tillet, Salamishah, 45
Tomlin, Mattson, 109. See also *Wrinkle in Time, A*
Tracy (*Project Power* character), 117–21
Trudy (writer and photographer), 64

US South: and *Beasts of the Southern Wild*, 100–101; Black girlhood in, 58, 69–78, 80, 93; Black men in, 50–52; and *Queen Sugar*, 66

violence: failure to protect against, 2–3, 155–60; in film, 96–97, 113, 134, 139–41; justification of, 41, 109–11; receptacles of, 100–104. See also abuse; bullying; sexual assault

Wallis, Quvenzhané, 99, 101
Warner, Kristen, 95
Webster, Crystal, 92
White, Emily, 72–73
white fear, 93, 98
White House, 17, 44, 45, 47, 56–59
white people: and colorblind casting, 89–93, 106, 121–22; and fast girls, 72, 80–81; as saviors, 93–98; in schools, 125, 132–133
white saviors, 89, 93–97, 109
white supremacy: and Black girls and women, 110, 147, 150, 152, 160; and Black men, 28, 156, 158;

white supremacy (continued) and Christianity, 70–71; and digital platforms, 48; and fast girls, 18. See also misogynoir
Winfrey, Oprah, 57, 65, 122, 125
Wink (*Beasts of the Southern Wild* character), 99–103
womanhood, Black, 8, 44, 54, 68, 108. See also Black women
Woman King, The (film), 148–49, 150
women. See Black women
Wrinkle in Time, A (L'Engle), 121–22, 153
Wrinkle in Time, A (film), 19, 108–10, 121–27, 153. See also Alex; Meg

Yee, Angela, 9–10
YouTube, 9, 48
Yung Miami, 54

Zeitlin, Benh, 100–102, 105. See also *Beasts of the Southern Wild*
zombies, 87, 88–90, 96. See also *Girl with All the Gifts, The*